RANI GAIDINLIU

Legendary Freedom Fighter from the North East

SOM KAMEI

PAPER MISSILE
NIYOGI BOOKS

Published by
NIYOGI BOOKS
Block D, Building No. 77,
Okhla Industrial Area, Phase-I,
New Delhi-110 020, INDIA
Tel: 91-11-26816301, 26818960
Email: niyogibooks@gmail.com
Website: www.niyogibooksindia.com

Editor: Sucharita Ghosh
Layout: Shashi Bhushan Prasad
Cover design: Anurag Hira
Cover illustrator: Douluri Narayana

ISBN: 978-93-91125-62-2
Publication: 2022
Reprint: 2023

Price: ₹299

Publisher's note: Every effort has been made to ensure the accuracy of the information presented in this book. The images used in this book come from either the public domain or from the public commons, unless otherwise stated. The publisher welcomes comments and feedback from readers, in order to improve future editions, at niyogibooks@gmail.com.

Printed at Niyogi Offset Pvt. Ltd., New Delhi, India

For

My Father
Professor Gangmumei Kamei
A Scholar, Humanist, Activist
and a Lifelong Seeker of Knowledge

CONTENTS

PROLOGUE

We know Rani Gaidinliu as a well-known freedom fighter today, remembered fondly by the people and given recognition and honour by the Government of India. Her struggles and legendary exploits against the mighty British Empire in North East India are well documented. Her contribution to the freedom struggle is being taught as part of the history syllabus in schools and colleges in India.

Some years ago, on 26 August 2015, the Government of India commemorated the birth centenary of Rani Gaidinliu culminating in a year-long celebration all over India. At the inauguration of the birth centenary celebrations at New Delhi's Vigyan Bhavan, Prime Minister Narendra Modi issued a commemorative coin of hundred rupees and a circulation coin of five rupees featuring Rani Gaidinliu (p.233). The prime minister credited Rani Gaidinliu with spreading the message of Mahatma Gandhi in North East India. Referring to her as 'Rani Maa', the prime minister said that it is our misfortune that people such as Rani Gaidinliu are not remembered adequately. He emphasised that the legacy of the struggles and achievements of our freedom fighters have to be passed on to the succeeding generations.

At the same function, Union Home Minister Rajnath Singh said that Rani Gaidinliu had won the love and affection of the people of the north east with her revolutionary zeal. The home minister also added that the recent peace accord with the National Socialist Council of Nagaland (Isak-Muivah) (NSCN[IM]) takes forward the dream of Rani Maa of securing peace and stability in the region. Finance Minister Arun Jaitley too spoke glowingly about the contribution of Rani Gaidinliu to the process of national integration. Jaitley said that with the celebration of the birth centenary of Rani Gaidinliu, one of the most fascinating stories of a revolutionary leader is being retold today. Chief ministers of Nagaland and Manipur, T.R. Zeliang and Okram Ibobi Singh, respectively, were present on the occasion and paid rich tributes to her memory. The Minister of State for Development of North East Region (DoNER) Jitendra Singh announced that as a tribute to Rani Gaidinliu, the DoNER ministry intends to create a library-cum-museum at Kohima which would be dedicated to her. Unfortunately, this announcement set off a chain of events back in the small state of Nagaland where social organisations representing various tribal groups, tribal councils and even religious organisations vehemently protested against the setting up of the library-cum-museum at Kohima. A war of words started in the local newspapers condemning the proposal to commemorate and honour her in Nagaland. The basic arguments against the move were based on the premise that Rani Gaidinliu was 'pro-India' and therefore 'anti-Naga' as she worked against the interest of Naga nationalist political groups who wanted an independent sovereign Nagaland. Also, since Gaidinliu promoted her own version of indigenous religion known as the 'Heraka' in an otherwise Christian majority state, she was seen as working against the interest of the majority religious groups in Nagaland. Allegations and vilification campaigns against Rani Gaidinliu followed this announcement by various pro-independence writers and retired bureaucrats egged on by vested interest groups. This continued for months. Most views expressed were jaundiced and biased, based on the writings of British colonial authors and on information passed on from their social milieu based on hearsay and rumours. Wild allegations flew thick and fast and I cannot even mention them here as some of the vitriolic comments were well below the belt. One interesting allegation was that it was a conspiracy by the rightist Rashtriya Swayamsevak Sangh (RSS) to promote Hinduism and proselytise Naga society. Nothing could have been farther from the truth.

I began to wonder why the personality of Rani Gaidinliu aroused such extreme reactions from different sets of people in North East India? These reactions from different quarters have confronted me as an author as I started to read more and delved into the enigmatic life of Rani Gaidinliu. Gaidinliu was simply known as 'Apei Rani' or Grandma Rani amongst her people, the Zeliangrongs, a proud and conservative tribe, inhabiting the once contiguous geographical area of Manipur north and west districts, Cachar district, parts of Barak Valley of Assam, and Peren district of Nagaland.

At this point, I must mention that ever since I was a small child, I had heard riveting stories about Rani Gaidinliu from my grandparents, who were both supporters of her movement, as well as from the elders of our small community. However, the real account of her exploits came from my father Professor Gangmumei

Kamei who himself met the legend on one of her visits to Imphal in the late 1950s. My father's first meeting with the Rani took place at Imphal in the late 1950s at his friend Ajang Gangmei's place in Kakhulong village. It seems his friend's father was the *khulakpa* (village chief) and he was hosting the Rani on one of her tours to Manipur. My father next got an opportunity to meet the Rani after many years when the chief architects of a separate Zeliangrong Administrative Unit persuaded my father, who was then a young social activist, to meet the Rani at Kohima. The team consisted of Shri Kamei Kakhangai, a former MLA, Shri Kalanlung Kamei, then president of the Rongmei Naga Association, and Mr Namgaheing of Naga Hills. My father accompanied the team to Kohima and met the Rani in 1966 after she decided to come overground. My father further recalled that the Rani was being put up in the official bungalow of Deputy Commissioner S.C. Dev. My father has written about this meeting extensively in his memoirs.

As far as I can remember, Rani Gaidinliu used to stop over in Imphal whenever she visited her village Longkao or Tamenglong HQ and she used to stay over in my parents' house during these occasions. As children we used to be really excited whenever she came visiting as she was very compassionate towards everyone, especially children. She was fondly called 'Apei Rani'. Personally, I had a very good rapport with her. She had even predicted that I would make something of my life and contribute to the Zeliangrong welfare. For me, the most vivid memory of the Rani's compassionate nature and her love for children remains her visit to New Delhi in 1986. She was staying in the Nagaland State Guest House located at Sector XII, R.K. Puram, just next to my boarding school. Even though many visitors had come to call on her, when she saw me, she called me to her room and asked me to close the door. Then from her little bag, she took out two hundred rupees and gave it to me as pocket money. She gave me her blessings and told me that whatever I become in life, I should always work for the glory of our God Tingkao Ragwang and for the betterment of our Zeliangrong people. For a young teenager like me then, the generous pocket money meant a lot more than her blessings and words of wisdom. But over the years, I realised that I was one of the lucky few who were fortunate enough to receive her blessings. I can now fathom how she could inspire everyone around her and they in turn were even ready to sacrifice themselves for the cause of the people. I had a firsthand experience of her ability to easily connect with any age group and it was obvious that she was not just a simple 'Apei' (grandmother) but a great motivator of men and women.

While my father's accounts helped me to draw up a picture of the Rani's continued political struggle for her people who found themselves displaced by narrow political boundaries and divided into three north-eastern states of India, I could not fully fathom the many social, religious, economic and political implications of her struggle for what she thought was right and just. She appeared to be a complex personality who not only played a historical role in the Indian freedom movement but also fought for the preservation of her indigenous tribal way of life against all odds thrown in her path by not just the British but also her own fellow Naga groups who were fighting for independence and for a sovereign Nagaland. I needed to rediscover her and take a hard, objective look at the stories by not only insiders, consisting mainly of political associates, sympathisers, supporters, documents going back to British rule by academicians who are both Indian nationalists and foreigners, but also her opponents (both ideological and political), and last of all descendants from her own family. In the surrounding cacophony, we cannot forget that she was a woman who grew up in a different social milieu where patriarchy was the dominant norm as in all tribal society. I hope my humble effort will lead to a better understanding of this legendary figure of history and clear doubts about her extraordinary life, what she stood for, ideologically, morally, politically and, most importantly, her unwavering strong stand on cultural and religious preservation of the indigenous tribal groups in the region and country as a whole.

THE GENESIS

Any story about Gaidinliu and her people automatically points to Jadonang as the genesis. Jadonang[1] (1905-1931) was a mystic rebel who was spiritually inspired to organise the religious and social reforms among the Zeliangrong Nagas of Assam, Manipur and Nagaland. He also visualised a kingdom (*Makam Gwangdi*) for his people which was described by the British colonial government as the 'Naga Raj'. His concept of *Makam Gwangdi* brought him to a headlong clash with the British government. He was also inspired by Mahatma Gandhi and the Congress movement for freedom. Jadonang was imprisoned at Tamenglong (Manipur) in December 1928 for prophesising the end of British Raj and the coming of 'Naga Raj'. The colonial authorities saw him as a threat because his idea

---

1 Gangmumei Kamei, *Jadonang: A Mystic Naga Rebel* (Imphal: Smt. G. Lanshailu Kamei, 1997).

challenged the legitimacy of the colonial power and his concept of *Makam Gwangdi* in a way was seen as a direct challenge to them. He was arrested for the alleged proclamation of Naga Raj and executed on the false charge of murder on 29 August 1931. Historians have regarded his Naga Raj movement as a part of the greater Indian tribal movement with millenarian elements against the colonial rule of the British. Social scientists also perceive Jadonang's *Makam Gwangdi* as an act of nascent nationalism that attempted to draw his people from across borders and establish a larger political unit or pan-ethnic identity. It was aimed at the creation of a fraternity, social unity and integration of the three main groups of Zemei, Liangmei and Rongmei including the Puimei group. This was also probably the first attempt amongst the Nagas to unite a community across borders in order to establish some form of a political unit through the concept of *Makam Gwangdi* before the Naga nationalist leader, Angami Zapu Phizo's call for pan-Naga unity for political independence in the 1950s.

After Jadonang's arrest and execution, the movement was carried on with greater vigour by his young and energetic, firebrand disciple Gaidinliu, then only 14 years old. She continued to defy British authority through anti-house tax movement and armed resistance movement in the Naga Hills region. This is where the story of Gaidinliu and her fascinating adventure begins.

The Ecological Settings

Historically, the Zeliangrong territory covered the whole mountain tract from the Dhansiri river in the north to the confluence of the Chin Hills of Burma in the south, from the Bhubon Hills, eastern Cachar plains of Barak Valley and hills of eastern Meghalaya in the west, to the Koubru-Laimaton range overlooking the beautiful Imphal valley to the Mao-Maram Hills in the east. The southern boundary since the middle of the 19th century according to British ethnographers was at latitude 24.70°N though the more accurate line is 24.30°N running across northern Churachandpur district of Manipur, from Bhubon Hills to Thangjing Hills. According to the English ethnographers like McCulloch, Brown and Hodson, the southern ethnic boundary of the Zeliangrong country was one day's journey to the south of Manipur-Cachar bridle path, popularly known as the Tongjei Maril in Manipur (the bamboo tube line, so called because of the narrow and precipitous topography of the path). The bridle path was improved by the British engineers in 1838-39 and converted into a motorable road during the Second World War. This little path was the silent witness to the changing fortunes of the Manipuri kings and rulers, the bloody encounters during the Burmese invasions in the 18th and 19th centuries, and it is one of the most important trade routes connecting Manipur valley with the rest of India.

The Zeliangrong habitat covering an area of more than 10,000 square kilometres is situated over the northern, southern and western branches of the great Barail range of the eastern Himalaya system. The stiff mountains, deep gorges and river valleys provide shelter, sustenance and protection to the ancestors of the Zeliangrong people who had moved into the region more than 5,000 years ago. The important hill ranges and peaks of the region which are interwoven with the myths and traditions of the people are the Paona and Peren ranges in the northern spurs of Mt. Zapfu in Nagaland, the Haflong slopes in the western spur of the great Barail ranges running southward from Mt. Essau in Mao area of northern Manipur connecting with the Koubru-Laimaton range and the Cachar plains. There are several ranges of varying sizes and heights. The traditional nine ranges between Manipur and Cachar begin from Assam, one having to climb up the low-lying Tausem or Vangai range and Nungjaiband, then crossing the Makru river, climbing up the Oinamlong or the Kala Naga range (3,600 ft), then making a descent down to the Barak river and climbing up the Kambiron (Jadonang's village), then to the Nungba range (3,250 ft), then marching to Mongjaron Khullen and making a descent down to the Irang and climbing up the Khoupum range west of the Khoupum valley, next climbing up the Napsinmei or Phourungba range (4,700 ft) and climbing down the Leimatak and then ascend to the Liematak-Ngariyal peak (5,600 ft) and down to Bishnupur in south Manipur valley. Some of the other peaks associated with legends and traditions of the Zeliangrong people are Gaidaibut, Pankibut, Khoupum, Kasuakbut, Hangrum and Kacha khou in northern Tamenglong.

The Barak and the Irang are the two important rivers in this region. The Barak, known as Ahu (meaning nature's tongue in Zeliangrong), and the Irang, known as Alang, are so intertwined with the folklore and worldview of the Zeliangrong people that poets and bards refer to Barak as Mother and Irang as Father. The Milky Way in the sky is described in folklore as the heavenly

Ahu and Alang. The Barak starting from Liyai in north Mao, traverses the whole Zeliangrong country down to Tipaimukh then running up to Jirimukh and then to Cachar where it turns into a demon of destruction and a creator of fertile soil in the Barak Valley. The Irang starting from the upper portion of the Koubru range falls into the Barak in Churachandpur district, the Dzuko which runs parallel with the Barak and Jiri flows into the Barak, the Makru flowing down from Zapfu peak also flows into the Barak. Other rivers like the Ijei (Aga) and Leimatak (Apin) flow into the Irang. The river basins of Ijei and Leimatak are very fertile areas; the Makru and Barak basins covering the whole Tausem sub-division are among the most inaccessible regions.

The beautiful Barak waterfalls (four steps falls) between Sempang and Makoi villages in Tamenglong district of Manipur and the four freshwater lakes on the west bank of the Barak, a few kilometres from the waterfalls, known as the Zeilad lakes are the source of myriad folktales. The region is also endowed with several natural caves, the famous ones being Tharon caves near Tharon village, water-formed sandstone caves and the holy cave in Bhubon Hills (Assam) considered a holy pilgrimage site for the Zeliangrongs discovered and popularised by Jadonang and Gaidinliu. The Zeliangrong region is thus endowed with rich natural resources, forests and ample water from the big rivers, and the fertile valley of Khoupum (Manipur) and the vast Zaluke valley (Nagaland).

Who are the Zeliangrongs?

In the ethnic landscape of North East India, the Zeliangrong people are a unique example of the evolution of a common identity of a group of cognate tribes who were, though of a common origin, separated by a hostile geography and history, followed by social non-communication and lack of common organisation, but now due to historical development or circumstances, the same people have been united by bonds of common origin, common kinship, common cultural heritage reinforced by the experience of shared suffering at the hands of alien invaders. The name 'Zeliangrong' is the combination of the prefixes of the cognate tribes namely Zemei, Liangmei, Rongmei and Puimei (ZE+LIANG+RONG) which was coined on 15 February 1947 to give a common name to the said group. This development amongst the Zeliangrong group was not just a coining of a new name but a self realisation and rejection of all the external names given by former rulers and neighbours such as Kabui (for Rongmei & Puimei), Kacha Nagas (for Zemei & Liangmei) by Manipuri kings and subsequently documented by the British and given official status in Independent India. In Nagaland, the Zemei and the Liangmei are clubbed together as Zeliang only. In Assam, the Zemei and the Rongmei are recognised separately. With this declaration and adoption of a new term 'Zeliangrong', there evolved a deep sense of unity and identity amongst the cognate groups. Moreover, many philologists like G.A. Grierson[2] have grouped the Zeliangrong with the Naga-Bodo linguistic sub-family and contemporary linguistic studies in India and abroad have firmly established this close affinity and common origin of the group.

Another linkage is the common social structure found amongst the Zeliangrong cognate groups. The Zeliangrong society is a patriarchal society with two moieties or major clans, namely the Pamei and Newmei, which are further subdivided into many exogamous clans and sub-clans. These two major clans are found

2 G.A. Grierson, (ed), *Linguistic Survey of India*, vol. 3, 'Tibeto-Burman Family, Pt. 3' (Calcutta: Office of the Superintendent of Government Printing, India, 1904).

in all the three cognate tribes, which are subdivided into clans with different names. The commonality of the origin of the clans can be seen in the fact that the major clans have a totem.[3] For example, the Pamei clan is found in the four cognate groups. Among the Rongmeis, the Pamei clan is divided into lineages like Kamei, Phaomei, Singongmei, Kamson, Malangmei, Khangdaimei, Thankang, Daimei and the Pamei. They all share one single totem, the wild green pigeon (*Ahuina*) which is forbidden food for all the clans and the sub-clans of the Pamei moiety. However, there are some exceptions like the Malangmei sub-clan who has the black monkey (*Paang*) or hornbill as their totem. The Newmei is also found amongst the four cognate groups; they are subdivided into Gonmei, Panmei, Remmei, Dangmei, Abonmei, Thaimei, Rongmei, Gonthangmei, etc. Kinship therefore is crucial in forming the ethnic identity of Zeliangrong.

The third instance of commonality amongst the Zeliangrong cognate groups is the strong sense of their past or history which can be seen in their myths and

3 Totem is a natural object or animal that is believed by a particular society to have spiritual significance and that is adopted by it as an emblem (source: Oxford English Dictionary).

legends carefully preserved in their rituals, hymns, songs, and oral traditions. History in all tribal societies is based on oral tradition handed down through generations. They believe their ancestors emerged from a mystical cave called Taobei which perhaps is a non-existent place. The Zeliangrong also believe that they sometime lived with other Naga tribes like the Mao, Tangkhuls, Semas, Angamis and the Chakhesangs, hence their clubbing of Zeliangrong in the Naga conglomeration. It also appears that the ancestors of the Zeliangrong were in contact with the Dimasa-Kacharis as evident from some folk songs.

It is believed that the ancestors of the Zeliangrong lived at Makhel, a village close to the Manipur-Nagaland border. From Makhel, they came to a deep gorge called Ramtin-Kabin where they took shelter for some time. Emerging from Ramtin-Kabin they came to settle down in a place which came to be known as Makuilongdi near the present Oklong village in Mao west in Manipur's Senapati district. They built a settled life based on shifting agriculture and it is believed that the village became very populous due to its prosperity. But due to the excessive pressure on land and perhaps some internal differences among the ruling clan, different batches of people migrated from Makuilongdi. From the two relics of small mounds of stones found at Makuilongdi named Pamei and Newmei stones, it is presumed that the people have developed into two moieties, the Pamei and the Newmei. Legend says that the sons of the chief of Makuilongdi settled down on the Koubru mountain. In Zeliangrong folklore, Koubru is called Ragwang Phaipa, the landing place of God. This group of migrants went to the northern and western slopes of the great Barail range in search of flatlands. They came to be known as the Zemei people or the dwellers of the plain and warm land. Another group went towards the south which was unoccupied barren land, the inhabitants known as Maruangmei which later on became corrupted into Rongmei. Those who stayed back at Makuilongdi and nearby areas came to be known as Liangmei, the northerners.

The southward migration of the people continued upto the confines of the Chin Hills of Burma and Mizoram covering the Churachandpur district in present-day Manipur. Even today, there are a large number of stone megaliths in the deserted or semi-deserted villages, relics of the Zeliangrong habitation. The southern Zeliangrong had to face the brunt of the migration of Kuki-Chin tribes from Burma into Manipur. The migration happened in batches of small groups over an extended period; thus came the Koms, the Koirengs, the Chirus, the Hmars and the Kharams who were known to the Zeliangrong as the Koumei. The Zeliangrong were further pushed up to the point which has been located by the British ethnographers at the latitude 24.70 north of the equator. There are innumerable stories of heroic fights taking place between the cultural heroes of the Zeliangrong folk and the Koumei intruders.

The Zeliangrong of the Barail range came into conflict with the Dimasa-Kacharis whose capital was at Dimapur in present-day Nagaland and later on at Maibong, North Cachar Hills and further moved to Khaspur in the Cachar plains. The Kacharis and their rulers tried to establish hegemony over the Zeliangrong people. There are various historical anecdotes about a fight between the Zemei hero Jamlenang and the Kacharis who ultimately killed him through a well-planned deceptive stratagem. The heroic fights, the courage and bravery of Jamlenang are preserved in popular traditional folk songs. Another folk tale refers to the Kachari king who abducted Rengsonnei, the beautiful wife of Nakam, whose tragic songs filled with anguish and sadness are sung even today.

The link between the Meitei people with those of Zeliangrong is quite ancient. The Meitei chronicles and historical texts of Manipur refer to the relations between the two peoples. As stated earlier, the Tamenglong hills, its stiff mountains and dense forests provided shelter to the fleeing Meitei princes during the repeated rebellions and invasions from Burma. The relationship between the Zeliangrong and the kings of Moirang in the southern Manipur valley are found in the *Khamba-Thoibi* epic of Moirang as well as in their folklore. There were repeated military conflicts between the Meitei rulers and the Zeliangrong villages of the Koubru-Leimaton basins. The Zeliangrong village chiefs helped King Garib Niwaz of Manipur during his exile and he also took shelter in the Zeliangrong country during his liberation struggles against the Burmese. Even today, there are relics connected with his sojourn in the Tamenglong hills. During the Burmese occupation of Manipur (1819-1826) which coincided with the 1st Anglo-Burmese War, the Zeliangrong people resisted the Burmese invaders and assisted the Manipur princes.

From contemporary accounts, it is clear that the Zeliangrong people of western Manipur were independent of any alien rule during this period.

R.B. Pemberton, a British officer who helped Raja Gambhir Singh in taking back Manipur from the Burmese has written about them in his accounts. It was Raja Gambhir Singh of Manipur who first introduced administrative authority over the southern portion of the Zeliangrong country along the three trade routes, the Akhui, the Cachar road and the Khongzai route. *Cheitharol Kumbaba*, the royal chronicle of the Manipur kings, records the military expedition of Gambhir Singh to the region. Pemberton writes about the situation unfolding in the early part of the 19th century,

> The whole tract comprised between the Khongzai route on the south and that of Aquee on the north is occupied by the Kaopooe (Rongmei) Nagas who are tributary of Manipur. Until the authority of Gambhir Singh has been fully established over them, they were engaged in a constant warfare; travellers dare not venture to pass through the country except in large bodies, even then, were compelled to pay largely at every place for permission to continue their journey. Now, however, they have been effectively subjugated that 'Dak men' locally traverse the whole country with perfect safety and no single

> instance that I am aware of, has occurred in the last several years of their being attacked, stopped or plundered.[4]

The British gradually started penetrating the northern Zeliangrong country 1832 onwards in connivance with the Manipur kings. E.R. Grange, widely known as the 'father of Assam Rifles', led the first expedition to Zeliangrong country. The Manipur sector of the Zeliangrong area was brought under British rule with their conquest of Manipur in 1891. The Zeliangrong people were opposed to the imposition of house tax on them. This led to disproportionate and exceptionally harsh military campaigns against the Zeliangrong, especially in north-west Manipur under the command of C.L. Crawford, assistant political agent of Manipur. During the Kuki Rebellion (1917-1919), the Zeliangrong villages of Manipur suffered the most due to British failure in providing protection to them, thus shaking the confidence of the people in British rule. After the Kuki Rebellion, the north-west sub-division was created with Tamenglong as the headquarter.

4 R.B. Pemberton, *Report on the Eastern Frontier of British India* (1835; Reprint: Gauhati, 1966).

Earlier in Assam, also, regular British administration was established in the Haflong area (at Asalu) and the Barema area of Naga Hills.

In fact, historian Gangmumei Kamei[5] considers the 18th century as a landmark period in the history of the Zeliangrong people. It was a significant period in which the fight of the Zeliangrong people against the foreign invaders was intense and disturbing with the appearance of the Kuki immigrants who were pushed out of the Chin Hills and Mizoram by the Lushai tribesmen. The Zeliangrong people also had to reckon with the powerful Meitei rulers of Manipur whose attitude continued to be one of contempt despite the Zeliangrong help at the time of crisis in their history, when the aggressive Angamis and migrating Kacharis established their capital at Maibong and Khaspur. They were engaged in a mighty resistance against the Kukis. To understand why the Zeliangrong people suffered and how they rose up in arms against the British rulers a little background on the Kuki Rebellion is necessary here.

It was officially stated that the Kuki Rebellion started as a violent reaction to the British recruitment of Kukis to

5 Gangmumei Kamei, *A History of the Zeliangrong Nagas: From Makhel to Rani Gaidinliu* (Guwahati: Spectrum Publication, 2004).

the Manipur Labour Corps No. 22 for service in France during the First World War (1917). The Nagas from the Naga Hills District, Mizos from the Lushai Hills district (now Mizoram) and tribal labour consisting of Nagas and Kukis were recruited. Political Agent J.C. Higgins, followed by his reliever Col. H.W. Cole, and Raja Churachand Singh of Manipur believing in the 'traditional friendship' between the government and the Thadou chiefs of the Kuki group resorted to persuasion for the recruitment to the Labour Corps. A first batch of 2,000 labourers consisting of 1,000 Nagas and 1,000 Kukis were recruited through the pressure exerted by Rev. William Pettigrew of American Baptist Mission of Ukhrul, and his Naga and Kuki converts led by Teba Kilong were sent to France in 1917. Trouble arose when the second batch of labourers was to be recruited. The Thadou Kuki chiefs were opposed to the idea because of a rumour spread by an interested Meitei leader of the difficulties and miseries to be faced on the trip to Europe. A pretender to the throne, Chingakhamba Sanajaoba encouraged the Kuki chiefs to rise up against the state. The Kuki chiefs were aware of the government's limitations due to the war unfolding in faraway Europe and took full advantage of it. They formed a confederacy to attack the British Government.

The Kuki rebels in course of their rebellion turned against the Nagas, especially the Zeliangrong in the north west of Manipur and the Tangkhuls in north-eastern Manipur and in some tracts of Upper Burma. This anti-Naga action was aimed at the establishment of the Kuki authority over the Nagas and the occupation of their land for cultivation by the Kukis. Though the Kuki Rebellion was anti-imperial and anti-monarchical, their anti-Naga military operation opened up a new front to fight and it proved to be disastrous for them. Among the Kuki-Chins, only the Thadou Kukis were involved and they happened to be a formidable force. The British organised a new command to deal with the rebellion and divided the military command into seven areas namely, Jampi Area, Henglep Area, Mombi Area, Burma Road, Chassad Area, North Tangkhul Area, and North Somra & Tezu River Areas. For the purpose of this narrative, focus is being confined to the Jampi Area (the area between the Barak river and Imphal-Dimapur Road with supply bases at Bishnupur, Henema and Tapon) which falls under the Zeliangrong country. There were four leaders of the rebellion in the Jampi-Khoupum-Loibol Area: the chief of Loibol, chief of Jampi, chief of Layang (Tingtong), and the masterbrain Enjakhup, an ex-sepoy of the Assam Rifles. Tingtong Haokip was a rash and intemperate chief. He negotiated an understanding with the Rongmei villages of Tamenglong, Akhui (Changdai), Khebuching (Puching), Wairangba, Rangkhong, Awangkhul (Longchum) and Lukhambi for a 'no war' pact between them. But there was an attack in Lukhambi village in which some Kukis were attacked and their guns confiscated but no lives were lost. Awangkhul and Rangkhong villages rushed to the aid of Lukhambi village. Tingtong retaliated in a most brutal manner by raiding Awangkhul when the male warriors were in the *jhum* fields and only womenfolk, mostly old women and children, were present and took the heads of 30 persons. This was the beginning of the Kuki-Zeliangrong conflict. The villagers of Awangkhul took shelter at Noney (Longmai) to the south of the Ijei river for about a year. Akhui, a powerful Rongmei village, retaliated by attacking a nearby Kuki village, killing a dozen Kukis. Tingtong, chief of Layang, swooped down on Akhui village and destroyed it by burning it to the ground and killing 76 persons.

The Government of Manipur instead of extending help to the Zeliangrong victims as their loyal state subjects, teased them, implying that this was a consequence of their own actions. This hurt the collective feelings of the Zeliangrong and aroused a strong community bond amongst them. Fifty Liangmei warriors of Lamlaba under the leadership of Dongkhal rushed to the rescue of the seized village. The Kuki raiders were successfully warded off and they beat a hasty retreat. However, it is pertinent to note that in some areas of the Zeliangrong country, such as in Khoupum and Nungba area, an understanding of peace and friendship between the Singsong Kuki chiefs and the chiefs of Rongmei villages was entered into for peaceful co-existence despite the pressure on the Singsong chiefs by the leadership of Tingtong Haokip and Enjakhup to attack the Rongmei villages. But overall there was a great sense of insecurity and restlessness in the Zeliangrong country due to the Kuki Rebellion. Hemmed in on all sides by hostile and powerful neighbours who wanted to dominate the Zeliangrong people to exploit their resources, they struggled valiantly to preserve their land. But the fighting was sporadic with village-level resistance. In the absence of a united tribal uprising, the Zeliangrong were subjugated. The 19th century was thus a century of pacification of the Zeliangrong people.

Against this backdrop of forced colonial subjugation of the Zeliangrong people, the rise of the Jadonang movement for 'Naga Raj' and subsequently Gaidinliu's taking over of the cudgel from Jadonang emerged as a challenge to British imperialism. This ushered in a new chapter in the social, cultural, religious and political resurgence of the Zeliangrong.

In this setting of turmoil, subjugation, poverty and social chaos, Gaidinliu came as a new hope and symbol of resistance against all the perceived injustices against the Zeliangrong people. The following chapters outline the story of Gaidinliu who later came to be known to the world as 'Rani Gaidinliu'—a term made famous by Jawaharlal Nehru in his writings who was touched by the stories of Gaidinliu during his travels in the North East before the independence of India.

MYSTICAL EARLY YEARS

In the late 19th and early 20th century, the Zeliangrong country was enveloped in the darkness of dire poverty. The British mercilessly exploited the impoverished people through the imposition of compulsory house tax, forced labour with no payments, and the most demeaning practice of porter subscription that was forced on all able-bodied men when the British officials passed through their villages. This forced labour conscription has been likened to slavery and it marked the nadir of the shameful British exploitation of the indigenous people of those times. Meanwhile, under the pretext of the Kuki Rebellion (1917-1919), which erupted primarily against the British surrounding the issue of recruitment of Kuki manpower for the Labour Corps during the First World War, some Kuki villages allegedly attacked Zeliangrong villages to settle 'old scores.'[1] Hence the Zeliangrong

1 N. Joykumar Singh, *Socialist Movements in Manipur (1917-1951)* (New Delhi: Mittal Publications, 1992).

became the unwitting victims of the backlashes of the marauding Kukis. The Kuki Rebellion made a huge impact on the psyche of the Zeliangrong people. After the British finally crushed the rebellion by brute force, they showed lenient clemency to Kuki immigrants to pacify the rebels. The Zeliangrong were spurred on to rise up against the British who were now seen as a collaborator of the Kukis.

In this period of gloom and suffering, the Zeliangrong people became more inward looking and were encumbered by superstitious beliefs and practices in everyday life. Moreover, the society was marked by inter-village feuds, disunity, unproductive lifestyles and general backwardness. In such a depressing scenario, the movement of Jadonang and his promise of *Makam Gwangdi* ('Naga Raj') provided a glimmer of hope for the Zeliangrong people. Though the Jadonang movement was nipped in the bud by the British by falsely implicating him in a murder and subsequently hanging him to death, Jadonang had managed to successfully light the spark of revolt against the mighty British. The enormous responsibility fell on the young shoulders of 14-year-old Gaidinliu who was already a full-fledged, trusted follower of Jadonang by 1928.

But who was Gaidinliu? Was she a priestess, a shaman or *maibi*, a mystic or simply a village girl inspired by Jadonang? Set in this background, this is a story of the extraordinary girl who was not literate in a modern sense but was truly aware of her people's plight and who simply decided to do something to mitigate the situation and change her world order. A change that brought hope and inspired her people to rise up in revolt against the injustices meted out to them. To find out how she accomplished this, one must undertake a journey to her village in Longkao, in the present Tamenglong district of Manipur.

Mystical Early Life

The Zeliangrong people are gregarious but at the same time very resilient by nature. The society was very democratic, more or less unlettered but rich in folklores, dance and song. The cultural heritage was something every Zeliangrong was proud of; it gave them a sense of identity and provided a strong historical foundation to deal with all odds thrown at them by unpredictable modern times. Myths and lores about their gods, goddesses, their origins, migrations, the heroes and heroines made their daily lives a little more interesting and bearable. One such Zemei myth tells a story that when the Almighty saw the sufferings of the people, he decided to send his daughter Cherachamdinliu to help and free the people from their life of bondage and sufferings. The Lord commanded his daughter to be born into the world in the womb of a mother named Kaluatlienliu, wife of Lothonang of Longkao village on 26 January 1915. This is one of the few known myths which has spawned over the years in all the cognate tribes of Zemei, Liangmei, Rongmei and Puimei.

One day in the early morning of 26 January 1915, a Thursday, Kaluatlienliu dreamt that two gigantic men were standing near her bed, but seemed to disappear into thin air just as she got up from her bed. She could not make out whether what she saw was a dream or an actual incident. In fact, the day was not a normal one, as the villagers also recalled sudden thunder and lightning without any prior warning like clouds gathering in the sky. These ominous signs made the people apprehensive and many villagers stayed back at home and refrained from working in the field that day.

In spite of all these unusual happenings Kaluatlienliu went to the nearby jungle to collect firewood but as soon as she returned home, she went into labour. There was no one in the house to help her, so she simply endured the pain associated with childbirth and gave birth to her baby girl. Kaluatlienliu noticed an exceptional phenomenon right after childbirth – her baby girl was looking at her with her eyes wide open. As it was the practice of the Zeliangrongs, the naming ceremony of the baby was held on the fifth day from the day of her birth, and she was named 'Gaidinliu', meaning the harbinger of good news in Rongmei dialect, by her aunts. Gaidinliu was the third daughter of Lothonang Pamei who had five sons and three daughters. Ramgonnang was the eldest son followed by Namkeliangpou (second son), Kiulianlu (eldest daughter), Lungthuidinnang (third son), Kiumanliu (second daughter), Lungloangam (fourth son), Gaidinliu (third daughter) and Khiusinnang (youngest son). The family belonged to the Pamei clan of Longkao village tracing their lineage to one Guangsuang Pamei who was considered the founder of the Longkao village or *khunbu* (landowner).

Gaidinliu was a tomboy, always ready to help her parents in their household work including the so-called men's work such as accompanying her father to the jungle in order to place animal traps in specific locations. In fact, she was like a lucky mascot for her father who felt that she brought good luck to their little expeditions. This was significant because in those superstitious days, the Zeliangrongs even had a saying that, 'If a girl or woman touches a trap before the trap is laid, the venture will be unfruitful.' In a sense, Gaidinliu's father was something of a pioneer in going against such sayings of those times. Going to the jungle with her father was one of Gaidinliu's favourite pastimes during her pre-teenage years. She was known to be a brave girl who was not afraid of anything even when she felt ill or sick and led a disciplined childhood obeying her parents. She was a simple girl who ate all kinds of vegetables cooked by her parents without any complaints. The Longkao villagers admired Gaidinliu for her gentle demeanour and good manners as she was ready to help not only her parents but also other villagers who needed errands run or required assistance.

Gaidinliu, like all children, had many friends and her best friend was a girl named Ramthonliu with whom she shared many extraordinary adventures as a child. Many of these stories about their adventures have been passed down in the village over the years and have now become a part of their folklore. Gaidinliu's bravery and fearlessness slowly started manifesting itself in many incidents even during her childhood. One such incident featured Ramthonliu who encountered a venomous snake during their daily collection of firewood in the nearby forest. Ramthonliu was numb with fear and remained immobile; it was the presence of mind of young Gaidinliu who immediately picked up a small twig and killed the snake that saved her best friend from any harm. Gangmumei Kamei in his early note on Rani Gaidinliu in the *Dictionary of National Biography*[2] (1972) described Gaidinliu as an independent and strong-willed girl, whose Amazonian way of doing things raised the eyebrows among the womenfolk of the village. For her, gender roles defined by tradition did not matter; she was more into getting things done by herself without depending on anyone else. Her mother was worried about her little daughter who was independent, determined and courageous, and persistent in whatever she did. She was the leader of the girls of her dormitory. There she exhibited her independence and a sense of equality. Once she wanted to visit the boys' dormitory hall. She was forbidden, as the girls are not allowed to visit the boys' dormitory. She vehemently protested and

2 S.P. Sen, ed., *Dictionary of National Biography* (Calcutta: Indian Institute of Historical Studies, 1972).

insisted upon visiting the boys' dormitory. Without realising it, she was a pathbreaker for gender equality in a traditional tribal society. To even think in a non-traditional way, defying age-old tradition and customs, was a luxury in such a strong patriarchal society like the Zeliangrong Naga community. Young Gaidinliu was far ahead of her times.

At the age of about 12 years, Gaidinliu along with Ramthonliu went to the *jhum* field of Gaidinliu's family to pluck green chillies. On their way to the field, a strange incident took place. A girl resembling Gaidinliu approached them. Ramthonliu whispered to Gaidinliu, 'Gaidinliu! Look at that stranger, who is she?' In fact, the stranger was a mirror image of Gaidinliu wearing the same clothes and looking exactly the same. The strange girl asked them in her calm voice whether she could accompany them to the *jhum* field to which both friends replied, 'Yes!', partly out of fear and partly out of extreme curiosity. The stranger replied, 'Then I will help you in plucking green chillies.' For the next few minutes there was absolute silence. It was a surreal scene, the strange girl was plucking chillies along with the two best friends. It is said that Ramthonliu could only make out who was the real Gaidinliu as she remembered that Gaidinliu had a mole on her hand which the stranger did not have. Soon the baskets were full, so it was time to go home. The girls started back for the village with their baskets full of chillies and the strange girl too started following them carrying her own basket of chillies. Gaidinliu and Ramthonliu looked hither and thither for familiar faces out of fear, trepidation and excitement but no one could be seen around. As they reached the foothill of the village, the strange girl distributed the chillies from her basket equally between the two friends and bid goodbye to them with a message that they should not speak about the encounter to any villager elder; it was to be a secret between them.

After this, the strange girl suddenly seemed to disappear into thin air. This frightened Ramthonliu and she rushed towards the village as fast as she could. As they were running towards their village, the two girls saw a wild cat (lynx) crawling by the pathway which also seemed to disappear into nothingness. At that moment, in the radiant twilight of the setting sun, both the girls ran as if their lives depended on it towards the safety of their respective homes. Being teenage girls, they were really excited and wanted to share the story of their strange encounter with their families but at the same time they dreaded the consequences of violating the warning issued by the stranger. Finally, they could not keep it a secret any more, and they spilled the contents of their strange encounter to Gaidinliu's mother. Both girls felt considerably lighter as if a huge burden had been lifted off their chests after sharing the story and it soon became part of the village folklore in later years. Legend has it that the strange girl was the daughter of Lord Bisnu (Mishnu in Zemei dialect), the head of the pantheon of gods of the Zeliangrong named Cherachamdinliu. In the Rongmei version it was the daughter of Lord Bisnu named Namgilu/Namginai who lives in the Bhubon cave in the Cachar hills. It is said that Gaidinliu's journey towards spirituality started with this incident. Thus began her lifelong struggle to forge a spiritual path in an organised way for the Zeliangrongs. It is believed that Namgilu and Gaidinliu shared a lifelong friendship and used to communicate regularly through various channels.

It is said that Namgilu's appearance in the Longkao village was with a purpose: an invitation to go to her father Lord Bisnu's abode in the Bhubon cave in the Cachar hills. Namgilu and Gaidinliu used to address each other as *Akalu* (my friend) and it is said that

Gaidinliu declined the invitation when she was first asked by her deity friend. Gaidinliu told her, '*Akalu*, I do not know the way that leads to your father's house,' but Namgilu insisted and reassured her that she will lead the way. Gaidinliu argued, 'I cannot go as you are a deity and I am a human being. It is not possible for human and deity to go together.' Even after hearing this, Namgilu was insistent and replied, 'You will not face any problem on the way as I will leave marks on the branches of trees on every path leading to my father's house.' After many reassurances from her friend, Gaidinliu finally decided to visit the Bhubon cave but only if her friends from Longkao village accompanied her. Her best friend Ramthonliu decided to accompany her on this important mission that would essentially determine Gaidinliu's destiny. The villagers decided that both the girls shall be accompanied by four able-bodied elders. This episode made many people amongst the Zeliangrongs justify that Gaidinliu was chosen by Tingkao Ragwang, the Almighty God, to lead her people and guide them towards a better life into a new horizon from the morass that they found themselves in.

But the question is, was it so easy for Gaidinliu to be accepted by the people of her community in an age and at a time when the role of gender was well defined and women were perceived as a weaker sex? Moreover, amongst the Zeliangrong there was a separate dormitory system (*Morung* system) for unmarried boys and girls where they are trained to face the challenges of life and survive in a hostile environment. The dormitory system was based on an age-set system where gerontocracy was strictly upheld. Gaidinliu not only overcame the accepted gender norms of those times but also the strict age-set based gerontocracy system and earned the respect of her elders by performing many extraordinary tasks and helping the people in general in times of sickness and difficulties. Many of the stories may have been a little exaggerated over the years but the point here is that it earned her respect and helped her gain the confidence of her people, a very important requirement when leading a movement or being accepted by everyone as a leader. For the benefit of the readers some stories are reproduced here as told to the author by associates and followers of Gaidinliu.

Her Association with Haipou Jadonang

The relationship between Jadonang and Gaidinliu was that of a master and a disciple. Gaidinliu first heard of

Jadonang of Kambiron village, known as a great *muh*, a religious prophet intent on reforming the Zeliangrong religion and bringing about unity among her people. She went to Kambiron to meet Jadonang in around 1926 to consult him about her dream divination and other problems besetting a young incumbent shaman (described by J.C. Higgins as a *maibi* or a priestess). It is said that Gaidinliu's family took her to Puilon village where Jadonang's temple was being built to consult him on the many dreams of Gaidinliu and her encounters with divine deities. They were concerned about Gaidinliu's well-being and wished to seek the opinion of Jadonang on her strange ways which no one in the village could logically explain. When young Gaidinliu met Jadonang, she recognised the spiritual power that Jadonang wielded. She wanted to learn from him and soon she became devoted to her master. Though their association lasted only four years, she soon became the most devout follower who could speak her master's language and understand his teachings. Jadonang knew that Gaidinliu was stubborn and headstrong though she was kind to everyone around her. She soon won his confidence and became a full-fledged *muhpui* after the performance of the ritual of *ralen loumei*, a propitiation ceremony.

Jadonang was preparing for a revolution for his *Makam* people and was busy training a youth force known as *Riphen,* consisting of both boys and girls. The duty of the *Riphen* included catching cattle, cultivation, pounding of paddy, collection of fuel and firewood, military training (wielding of *daos,* spear hurling and gun shooting), and gunpowder making for the muzzle loaders. They also accompanied their leader during his pilgrimage to the Bhubon cave and Zeilad lakes. They participated in the religious sacrifices, congregation, dancing and singing. It is said that at the peak of Jadonang's activities, the *Riphen* consisted of 500 members. Several villages sent their quota of *Riphen;* for example, Keikao village sent 15, Thingou village sent four, and many Zeliangrong villages did likewise. One of the main duties of the *Riphen* was to perform military drill with words of command coined by Jadonang.

Gaidinliu became a frequent visitor to the temple of Jadonang. She soon took up the responsibility of training the girls in the work of the *Riphen* (warrior). Their training consisted of singing and dancing 'the Jadonang dances and songs', sending secret messages, counting people in secrecy, calling names by code words, etc. Jadonang established alliances between villages for rebellion against the British by sending out a spear each to the villages for allegiance. If the spear was accepted, it meant the acceptance of the plan for the kingdom and it was celebrated with a feast, a *mithun*[3] being submitted as tribute to Jadonang.

Gaidinliu was greatly impressed by Jadonang whom she addressed as *Achại* (elder brother). Many writers have written that they were brother and sister. While Jadonang belonged to the Malangmei clan, Gaidinliu belonged to the Pamei clan. Both belonged to the Pamei or Kamei phratry; in that sense they could be called cousin brother and sister. Jadonang's pet name for Gaidinliu was 'Adinna'. Very often she visited Kambiron and Jadonang visited Longkao. A deep partnership blossomed between master and disciple while Gaidinliu's strong devotion to Jadonang's teachings and Lord Bisnu made her very popular amongst the followers of Jadonang. Ultimately, she became the most trusted lieutenant of Jadonang.

3 *Mithun* is a semi-wild bovine whose scientific name is *Bos frontalis*. It has great cultural significance amongst the tribes of North East India and South East Asia, usually used for sacrificial purposes and feasts of merit.

The Legend of the Divine Python

Gaidinliu was believed to communicate with the divine spirit quite frequently and could foretell many incidents especially sickness or tragedy or important events. Many early British writers have dubbed her as a shaman priestess or *maibi* in the local Manipuri dialect or a medicine woman. And the story that she could talk to gods and even animals spread quickly amongst the people. This was reinforced by her prediction that a python was lying in the hollow tree of *Nkuangbang* on the western side of the village as told by the divine angel in her dream and that it was to be brought to the village. The sceptical villagers went to check at the spot mentioned in the dream and to their utter surprise, they found a large python lying there. Now they were scared to even touch it and returned empty handed to the village. This was reported to Gaidinliu who told them to bring back any leaves lying around the hollow tree. So the village youths went back and brought the leaves as directed. Gaidinliu invoked a prayer on the leaves and put them inside a bamboo basket and advised the villagers to place the basket in front of the python. As directed by her, the basket was taken back to the hollow tree and kept in front of the python and it simply crawled into the basket.

The youth were again faced with a dilemma: who will carry the basket? It is said that a brave volunteer by the name of Agakdui carried the basket to the village. The story also says that the still sceptical villagers wanted to test whether the python was an ordinary one or whether it was indeed the one with divine powers. So they decided to set it free in the middle of the village and egged the python on to find his master's house. To their amazement, the python went straight to Gaidinliu's house and remained coiled under her bed. It was said that whenever domestic animals such as pigs, dogs, chicken, cats, ducks or goats ventured close to the python's whereabouts, they immediately stopped as though they were under a hypnotic spell. Such incidents attracted many visitors not only from within the village but from other nearby villages too. This caused a lot of disturbance in their daily lives. After a few days, nine days to be precise, Gaidinliu was told by her divine companion that she should return the python. Hence a prayer was performed at the residence of Gaidinliu and the next day, on the tenth day of the python's stay in the village, it was found missing. It was later revealed that the python was the Zeilad deity. Nobody knew what the purpose of the python's visit was. Only Gaidinliu seemed to know the real purpose of the strange visit.

An incident in the village was narrated to the author by Shri Abuan Kamei, the former personal assistant to the Rani till her demise in 1993, who was privy to many tales and stories about the Rani not known outside the immediate circle. One such incident took place during the divine python's stay at the village. The presence of the godly python had made the villagers very alert as they did not want untoward things to happen to any of the villagers. In the midst of all these, a childbirth took place in the village and all the relatives and midwives gathered in the house tending to the expectant mother. The birth process dragged on till early next morning and in the early break of dawn, a girl child was born to the mother. As soon as the baby was born the midwives heard some loud sound without so they went outside and were amazed to see Gaidinliu flying past the house. Her voice rang out loud and clear asking them to name the baby 'Digoliu' and then she suddenly disappeared. A search party comprising the village youth was sent to look for Gaidinliu and she was found lying on the ground near the entrance of the village. It was said that she emitted a strange, unearthly smell. Abuan Kamei further narrates that the girl Digoliu (Digoliu was also the name of one of the daughters of the Zeilad deity) grew up in the village and passed away only in the late 1980s.

Gaidinliu later recalled that Namgilu appeared before her and told her that the Zeilad deity was very pleased with her devotion to the python and that she was reaching a state of perfection. The story of the python in a way legitimises the rise of Gaidinliu and her acceptance by her followers as the chosen one anointed by divine power. In Zeliangrong folklore, the python is looked upon with awe since certain mythical powers are attributed to it. This can be seen in the story of Sa/Asa and Michurung (Munserung in Zemei dialect), popular folk heroes of the Zeliangrong. Popular because of their selfless deeds, they are often portrayed as mischievous and playful. They are portrayed in different guises: warriors, blacksmiths, jokers, kings and so on. In one such story, Asa and Munserung met on the banks of Zeilad lake and started producing iron. The python king inside the lake was irritated with the constant banging and instructed his minions to go and stop this noise. Seeing the pythons, Asa and Munserung immediately caught them, roasted their flesh and ate them. With none of the pythons left, and the noise still continuing, the python king surfaced in anger. He swallowed Munserung and returned deep inside the lake. Asa then devised a plan to drain the water of the lake and rescue his friend Munserung. He succeeded in draining the lake till the python king was visible. Asa threatened to kill and eat the python king if Munserung was not released. The python released Munserung and, out of fear, the python king also gave Asa and Munserung two gifts: a magic sword that kills any living being if used along with the word *hingpeubila* (an ancient untranslatable word), and a magic spear that also kills anything with the help of the word *di (*also untranslatable).[4] According to legends of the Zeliangrong, there is a magical rope called *pipereu* inside the Zeilad lake along with the gun-like weapon that Gaidinliu found in the Bhubon cave. Hence pythons are seen as keepers of weapons and arms for safekeeping in the Zeliangrong myths. Gaidinliu using the python in her narrative was therefore easily acceptable to her people. It was obvious that young Gaidinliu knew things that ordinary people could not even imagine or understand.

---

4 Sujata Miri, *Liangmai Nagas: Legends and Stories* (New Delhi: Vikas, 1991).

The Bhubon Cave and its Symbolism

The Bhubon cave is an important pilgrimage centre for the followers of Heraka (founded by Rani Gaidinliu) and every year during the month of January-February pilgrims from all over the region visit the cave. For the Heraka, the cave represents the point from where the reform began during the 1920s, as their God Tingkao Ragwang/Tingwang instructed the first reformers. The pilgrimage also reiterates their bond with the 'essence' of what Heraka is: the cave was the place where the blessing of God was bestowed upon Jadonang and Gaidinliu (the first Heraka reformers) who were then instructed to teach the Zeliangrong people. Many pilgrims have shared their accounts of the awe-inspiring influence of the cave on them, the supposedly miraculous effects it has had on them, and the immense power of the journey. The pilgrims believe that one of the most important and auspicious events for the Heraka is the pilgrimage to the cave and it is said that, ideally, one should visit the Bhubon cave at least thrice in one's lifetime.

Visit to Bhubon Cave in September 1927

With the assurance of her guardian angel Namgilu/ Cherachamdinliu, Gaidinliu set out on her journey to the Bhubon cave in the Cachar district of Assam along with her friend Ramthonliu accompanied by four elders of the village early one morning in September 1927. As promised by her guardian angel, Gaidinliu and her party could easily find their way safely to the Bhubon cave on the third day of their travel. This journey may also be considered as the first pilgrimage of Gaidinliu to the Bhubon cave, the godly abode of the Zeliangrong pantheon of gods.

On their arrival at the entrance of the cave the weary travellers found that the cave entrance resembled the *Hangseuki* (in Zemei) or *Tarangkai* (in Rongmei)—Naga male dormitory—except that it was naturally carved out of the rocks in the Bhubon Hills. The magnificent Bhubon cave faces the eastern side and there is also a portico or a verandah-like space just like the ones adorning houses of ordinary people. The awestruck visitors to the cave noticed that it had two entrances and it was later revealed that one was for Gaidinliu and the other entrance was meant for Jadonang. The doors according to folklore were made of stone and they opened and closed on their own and were guarded by armed sentries. Once the visitors pass through the gates, they encounter a stiff layer of stone having two rows of stones like armed benches for resting, and just after this climb they come across a vale-like hall where at least a thousand people can be accommodated. Just behind the vale of the hall, there is a stagnant pool inside the cave. The cave was inhabited by huge numbers of bats and it is believed that white bats (albino bats) are also found there. The appearance of white bats had a special significance for the visitors. On the walls of the cave, there are some engraved indecipherable scripts which the Zeliangrong people believed to be the scripture ordained by the Almighty God, Tingkao Ragwang. It was believed that those scripts could be read by Jadonang and Gaidinliu alone. It is said that the scripts reflect the problems of the earthly world and that all good and bad news can be learned through the scripts.[5]

When Gaidinliu and her party reached the main gate to the cave, they were confronted by a giant-sized man with a rifle-like weapon who blocked their path and spoke to them in a baritone voice saying, *'Cheduira panglang Kumla men, kamchelame, chethiu thiu, awaniye, kam kam shai lak ye.'* In the meantime, Gaidinliu was looking

5 The original scripts preserved in a notebook found with Gaidinliu when she was arrested are now preserved in the Pitt Rivers Museum Archive, Oxford. (Please see the photos at the end of the book.)

for her guardian angel Namgilu on whose invitation she had made this journey. She was delighted to see her standing near the entrance of the gate and asked her what the meaning of the sentry's question was. Namgilu, the friendly deity/angel, translated and interpreted the meaning. She said, '*Akalu*, the guard is asking, for what purpose have you entered this House? Either to kill or yield is my command.' Gaidinliu replied, '*Akalu*, we are invited by your kind grace and have come here to offer prayer to our Lord with a hope to gain good knowledge, but not to die.' After this quick-witted answer, the guard allowed them to enter the cave generally believed to be the abode of Lord Mishnu/Bisnu. This is not to be confused with the Hindu pantheon god Vishnu.

The Pilgrim's Encounter at the Bhubon Cave

After the intervention of the friendly deity Namgilu, Gaidinliu and her party were allowed to enter the hallowed abode of the gods. Overwhelmed by the situation and the surreal surroundings, Gaidinliu led her party in while singing the devotional song '*Ragwang Damtuang/Jug-Neipuiluh*' ('Psalm of Glory' composed by Jadonang – see Appendix-I) in praise of Tingkao Ragwang, the Almighty God. It is believed that this pilgrimage decided the course of Gaidinliu's future. She consciously promoted the ancient traditional religion of the Zeliangrong people and made it her lifelong mission to work for its growth and reformation. Gaidinliu was advised to visit again on her birthday which falls on 26 January as she had now come to know of the holy place of Lord Bisnu/Mishnu. Gaidinliu expressed her wish to bring a flawless *mithun* to offer in the sacrificial ceremony on her next visit but she was worried that it might raise eyebrows, especially from government officials, as this period was around the time when Jadonang had started his movement for *Makam Gwangdi* or Naga Raj for breaking the shackles of colonialism and consequently tight security was prevalent around the Zeliangrong region. She shared this anxiety with her kindly deity Namgilu who told her not to worry and gave her assurance that she will guide them to safety. Satisfied that the visit to the Bhubon Hills had been an eye-opening experience for her and her party, they set off on their return journey to her village, Longkao.

Once Gaidinliu got back from her pilgrimage, she performed the ceremonial house construction of *Taraang Kai* at Longkao. She immediately set about organising and setting up the *Kalum Kai/Kelumki* or the sacred shrine in her village where prayers and rituals were performed in honour of Tingkao Ragwang/ Tingwang. Gaidinliu and her friends started building for the first time a place of worship by constructing a platform with a raised monolith facing the Bhubon Hills and organised daily prayers in the morning and evening. Here hymns composed by Jadonang and some by herself were regularly sung for the first time. The practice of washing oneself before praying to symbolise purity of mind and body were adopted by the devotees. All these practices were new to her people but they happily adapted them in their daily lives. The *Kalum Kai* became a sacred space in the village and a better one was built like an altar with a four-foot-high monolith which was erected by the villagers of Longkao for praying for their well-being. The believers learnt new devotional songs and folk dances composed by Jadonang while Gaidinliu taught and preached about the primordial religion of the Zeliangrong. Thus Longkao village became a centre of social, religious and cultural revival. Gaidinliu immersed herself as a participant in the reformation movement of the Zeliangrong religion by seeking abolition of *Gennas* (prohibitions), organisation of religious congregations, performance of traditional dances and religious songs/hymns.

Being a follower of Jadonang, she was opposed to the oppressive rule of the British, especially the forced labour. This may have been because as a young girl she was also forced to carry the baggage of the government employees in her baskets. Gaidinliu came into contact with a large number of people from the three cognate groups of the Zeliangrong, from Assam, Imphal valley and Cachar valley. Guided by Jadonang and Lord Bisnu, she became even more determined to serve her people.

Second Visit to Bhubon Cave (26 January 1929)

Finally, the time to revisit the Bhubon cave as directed by the deity came, so Gaidinliu along with her friend Ramthonliu and four elders of Longkao namely Maliangban, Kanung, Ramlennang and Meijuding, started their journey for Bhubon Hills with a very healthy and flawless *mithun* on the morning of 23 January 1929. As predicted by the deity, they seemed to be guided by an unseen force on their way to the Bhubon Hills. On their way they met some policemen and government officials but it is said that whenever they were asked about the *mithun* accompanying them, they seemed to fall into some sort of a trance and quickly forget about it. This may or may not be true but there is no doubt that Rani Gaidinliu and her party safely reached Binakandi village, which lay near the foothills of the Bhubon Hills on 24 January 1929, without facing any obstacles posed by government officials or the police along with the sacrificial *mithun* accompanying the party. There are eyewitnesses in Binakandi village who can vouch for it. Gaidinliu and her party spent the night at Binakandi village and set off for the Bhubon cave the next day after offering prayers at the *Kalum Kai* said to be constructed under the guidance of Jadonang during his earlier visit to the village. They reached the Bhubon Hills on the evening of 25 January and halted the night at Gairiamnang Taobut. The next morning, i.e., on 26 January 1929 which is also Gaidinliu's birthday, they went down to the Bhubon cave and performed the sacrificial ceremony with the flawless *mithun* in a befitting manner as guided by the kindly deity. It is said that Gaidinliu prayed for the well-being of the Zeliangrong people and asked for the blessing of the Almighty Tingkao Ragwang for her long-suffering people in order to fulfil their collective aspirations.

Pautanzan Newme,[6] a lifelong follower of Heraka and Gaidinliu, translated the prayers of Gaidinliu. It goes something like this:

> Oh, Heavenly Father, the creator of the Sun and the Moon and all creatures. The biggest and the strongest of all Gods, known to the good and the bad of the universe (world). We are always under your tenderly care, please have mercy upon us by hearing the words of the unwise woman like me. The sustainer and the Protector of all of us, Oh! Tingwang, You are aware that the Zeliangrong people are your children but they are living under the administration of others in destitution till today. And we could not forebear the hardship imposed on the traditional tenets of our forefathers due to excessive suppression by our opponents and that has hindered us from developing our culture and traditions. Do protect us from all oppressive forces of evil from different corners to eliminate poverty and unsuitable tenets of the prophetic belief in Zeliangrong Society.

6 Pautanzan Newme (late) was the General Secretary of Zeliangrong Heraka Association, North East India.

According to Pautanzan Newme, this was the most significant visit of Gaidinliu to the Bhubon cave as it is believed that divine laws and teachings of Tingkao Ragwang/Tingwang was given to her for sharing amongst her people for fulfilling the aspirations of the Zeliangrong people. It later on laid the foundation for religious reform movements like 'Heraka' and 'Tingkao Ragwang Chapriak'. The basic tenets of the Zeliangrong religion as revealed to Gaidinliu by the Almighty Tingwang/Tingkao Ragwang were as follows:

1. Tingkao Ragwang/Tingwang created the universe and everything in it, so believe in Him and sing His praise and pray to Him.
2. The Sunrise prayer should be performed by chanting Tingwang/Tingkao Ragwang's name.
3. The birth and death ceremony were to be performed for all believers. Gaidinliu was told that as soon as a baby was born, it was to be named and the performance of the naming ceremony—*najung gaimei/ngau be mai*—was to be done on the fifth day. Feasts associated with birth and especially at the time of death are to be cut down.

4. Respect your parents and elders and preserve the good Zeliangrong culture.
5. Have a disciplined mind and a clean body. Selflessness and giving ways will make your image wonderful and you will become the son/daughter of Tingwang/Tingkao Ragwang.
6. In all speech and work, your mind must be truthful. Search for knowledge and light but breed not jealousy and enmity.
7. Love all of Tingwang's/Tingkao Ragwang's sons and daughters and search the way for happiness and peace.
8. Observe full moon day (*Jalua/Purnima*) well.
9. Set up *Kalum Kai/Kelumki* (house of worship) in all villages of the followers and pray with empty hands.
10. Have faith in rebirth.

It is believed that Gaidinliu asked many questions relating to traditional practices of the Zeliangrongs. She asked the deity, 'There are so many rituals and festivals in a year. Do we have to observe and celebrate all of them?' The deity replied, 'Let the most important festivals be observed and other ineffectual rituals and festivals are to be abolished. But the year-ending harvest festival "Gan-ngai" or "Hega-ngi"/"Chaga-gadi" must be observed and performed as it signifies the end of the agricultural cycle and a beginning of a new year which should be accompanied by prayers for good bounty and healthy life.' In the above festival, the last farewell rituals for the souls who left for their heavenly abode in the previous year are also performed. Therefore it has spiritual implication for the loved ones and hence its strict adherence during 'Gan-ngai/Hega-ngi.'

The above tenets of the Zeliangrong religion formed the foundation for becoming a more organised primordial religion later on under the leadership of Rani Gaidinliu—the reformed Heraka practice and later a reformed religion like Tingkao Ragwang Chapriak (TRC).

After these intense revelations interspersed with prayers, Gaidinliu was now rejuvenated enough to undertake the immense task of social, religious and cultural revival movement amongst her Zeliangrong people. The next day, i.e., 27 January 1929, Gaidinliu and her party descended the hills of Bhubon and halted again at Binakandi village and safely reached her village, Longkao, on 29 January. After that, without wasting any time, Gaidinliu started preaching these tenets in the form of rituals, songs, dances, prayers and hymns to all Zeliangrong people. What was even more admirable about Gaidinliu was that all these activities were carried out under her leadership when she was just 14-15 years old. Slowly and gradually the news of Gaidinliu and her messages of reform reached out to all Nagas especially amongst the Zeliangrong kindred tribes in the present states of Assam, Manipur and Nagaland.

Third Visit to Bhubon Cave (26 January 1930)

After year-long activities promoting and popularising the reformed primordial Zeliangrong religion in the countryside, it was again time for another pilgrimage to God's abode in Bhubon cave. Gaidinliu's social and religious reform movement provided a strong sense of belonging especially amongst the Zeliangrong kindred tribes and devotees from Assam, Nagaland and other parts of Manipur. They gathered at Longkao village to hear the preachings of Gaidinliu and learn new songs, dances and hymns being taught by her in praise of Tingkao Ragwang/Tingwang. A strong sense of pride was inculcated in the people as they proudly flaunted their association with the new reform religion which had a clear set of tenets preached by Gaidinliu.

For the visit to Bhubon cave, there were many volunteers who wanted to accompany Gaidinliu for the pilgrimage. It is said that Gaidinliu selected four young girls said to be virgins and set out for the pilgrimage along with all the followers which included volunteers from different parts of the Zeliangrong country. Here, also, the best-looking *mithun* said to be donated by Ketang village was taken along for ceremonial offering to God. The pilgrims halted the night at Kaiphundai village and the next day at Binakandi village (25 January 1930). The party reached their destination on 26 January 1930, on Gaidinliu's birthday. It was a beautiful sunny morning when Gaidinliu led her followers to the entrance of the cave and, as they were nearing the gate, a large rock is said to have opened out of nowhere. Once inside the cave, the party quickly got the *mithun* washed and cleaned, after which everyone got ready to offer prayers to Tingkao Ragwang. Though there were devotees in hundreds, there was pin-drop silence and a surreal atmosphere seemed to bedazzle the pilgrims. An amazing and dramatic scene was said to have played out. Even though they were inside a cave, a series of lightning flashes struck, one after another, and a godly figure seemed to appear at the door. Though many pilgrims did not see or feel anything, it was believed that some actually saw with their own eyes what transpired around them. The explanation given by the narrators was that only those who had a pious and pure soul were able to experience the amazing happenings around them.

After the prayer, the *mithun* was offered as sacrifice and hymns composed by Gaidinliu in praise of Tingwang were sung. It was revealed that the Lord Tingwang was very pleased by the prayers of the Zeliangrong people, so He has decided to send a gift to them. The gift was to be searched for by praying with closed eyes and whoever found it, had to share it with the whole community. A person named Lingtuang from Longkao village seems to have found it when he picked up a rifle-like object, around five feet long and deep red in colour. It was a heavy object which the volunteers carried to Gaidinliu who instructed all present to pray in thankfulness by singing the hymn '*Ragwang Damtuang*' and then they set off on their return journey. There are many versions of this story amongst the three kindred tribes. One version, as narrated by late Pautanzan Newme, says that while the men accompanying Gaidinliu carried the blessed weapon, a mysterious spell seems to have overcome them and they would lose their way, but as soon as they put it down, they were again able to regain their sense of direction. Another version said that whenever the weapon was carried, the party would hear animals like tigers roaring as if they were following the party, hence the people became very tense and worried about going further ahead with the weapon. To overcome these obstacles, Gaidinliu performed a sacrifice of a goat near Thangkim village (now Kahaoluang village) for the safety of the followers. After offering this sacrifice, they were able to finally reach Puilon village, the village of Jadonang, on 29 January 1930 in the late evening.

When they reached the village, Gaidinliu went to tell Jadonang about the incident.[7] That night both of them had a dream where Tingwang instructs Jadonang to shoot at the *Hebuibang* and Gaidinliu at the *Njingchibang* (a fruit-bearing tree). The story further describes the trials of the weapon in which Jadonang missed his tree trunk while Gaidinliu could hit the tree trunk and completely destroy it by firing at it. The narrators of the story in various versions emphasised the divine power of the weapon which could destroy a huge tree with a single shot. It was said that Jadonang was

---

7 Arkotong Longkumer, *The Poetry of Resistance – The Heraka Movement of North East India* (Guwahati: NESRC, 2016), p. 175.

urged by the elders of the village to try one more time to hit the target but he refused by saying that it was the will of Tingkao Ragwang that he missed, hence he will not try again as per His wish. This was also taken as a sign by the followers of Gaidinliu that she has been chosen as the leader of the Zeliangrong group for leading the social-political movement of the people.

These stories, in a way, legitimise and strengthen the acceptability of Gaidinliu as a leader. The story as narrated above can also be interpreted as a metaphorical one in which the giving of the mythical weapon by Tingkao Ragwang/Tingwang can be taken as a sign of anointing both the leaders as the chosen ones by arming them with divine wisdom and power for facing the enemies and obstacles in a very difficult situation which the Zeliangrong community as a whole found themselves in.

Thereafter, Gaidinliu returned to her village, Longkao, and the Zeliangrong kindred tribes from Assam, Manipur and Nagaland flocked to her village for a glimpse of Gaidinliu and to listen to her preachings. She started healing, prophesising and preaching about the new religious teachings received from Tingkao Ragwang in the Bhubon cave. Her activities were also legitimised by the curious arrival of Goddess Namgilu/Namginai who came riding on a lion pushed by the wind of God. The goddess was said to have arrived at Gaidinliu's house, drank water from the pond and rode away to the Nsimbutlua mountain. The people were somewhat frightened of these powers and regarded Gaidinliu as the reincarnation of the goddess.[8] She became a household name in the Zeliangrong country and believers from far and wide came to her for advice and to listen to her teachings. Many elders and learned people of the Naga community came to her to discuss and seek advice on ways to uplift the Zeliangrong society and bring about changes in their conditions. Gaidinliu propagated the reformation of the old sacrificial practices of *Paupaise* (*Pupou chapriak*) or old practices by adopting a simpler and purer form of worship of Tingwang or Tingkao Ragwang called the 'Heraka' religion. She also strongly motivated the believers to take up arms and overthrow the British rule by propagating the ideology of Jadonang's *Makaameirui Gwangtupuni* or self-rule by the *Makam* people which the British writers have termed as 'Naga Raj'. Hence her socio-religious reform movement had a strong political connotation which ultimately brought her in direct confrontation with the colonial rulers of those times.

8 Ibid., p. 176.

The Fourth and Last Pilgrimage to Bhubon Cave (26 January 1931)

It is said that both Jadonang and Gaidinliu had a vision in their dreams in which Tingwang directed them to come to the Bhubon cave together as there was an important message to be conveyed to them for the welfare of the *Makam* people. Accordingly, Gaidinliu along with about 400 devotees left Longkao village and camped at the foothill of Oinamlong village on 23 January 1931. Jadonang was also to join them there but since he was not there, two messengers were sent to Puilon village to convey that Gaidinliu and her 400-strong pilgrims' party were camping there waiting for Jadonang.

Meanwhile, Jadonang was celebrating the *Chaga-Ngai* festival in his village. When the two messengers came to him, he replied that he would join Gaidinliu and her party later as it would be rude to leave the festival in the midst of the celebration. So the next day, Gaidinliu started for the Bhubon Hills and Jadonang too started from his village along with his party of 50 men. However, both parties of pilgrims reached Bhubon Hills around the same time on 25 January 1931. The next morning, after sunrise, Gaidinliu and Jadonang along with their respective followers went to the cave. As they reached their respective gates, Gaidinliu's gate opened up and she entered with her followers but Jadonang's door remained closed and did not open up. Gaidinliu and her followers were already inside waiting for Jadonang to join her but after waiting awhile, she decided to start performing her prayers by singing the prayer hymns. Jadonang was waiting for his gate to open but since it did not, he also decided to use Gaidinliu's gate.

Once inside, Gaidinliu and her party were in the midst of singing the hymn '*Ragwang Damtuang*' for the third time when Jadonang and his followers entered and he rebuked Gaidinliu for not waiting for him. Moreover, he accused her of giving a false report about him to the Almighty and he insisted that was the reason why the cave door meant for him did not open. Jadonang went further and claimed that he discovered the holy cave when no one knew about it. He also claimed that it was he who levelled the foundation, erected the pillars, and kept the house in order before anyone else did. At this rebuke, Gaidinliu replied, '*Achai* [Elder brother]! Disgracing me in the midst of everyone is not good. If there are no roofings over the wooden posts and pillars it will decay by sun and rain, remember fire cannot defeat water. I don't deny that you are the beginner and discoverer of this holy place. Nor did I say a single wicked word against you.' It seems Jadonang's elder brother whispered to Gaidinliu that his brother was still under the influence of the *Chaga* festival merry making and requested her to forgive him. The bickering between the two leaders made the pilgrims uneasy and tense.

At that point, the Deity was said to have appeared and directed them to stop. The Deity proposed that the Zeliangrong country will be divided between the two leaders, demarcating the region north-east of the Barak river for Jadonang, and the region west of the Barak for Gaidinliu. At this intervention, Jadonang remained silent but Gaidinliu courageously replied to the Deity that she will not accept such a suggestion and will never allow the division of *Makam* or Zeliangrong's country. At this reaction of Gaidinliu, all the elders present there agreed and clapped their hands in support of Gaidinliu. It showed that Gaidinliu was a protagonist for Zeliangrong unity, something she fought for all her life. After this intervention, Jadonang and Gaidinliu reconciled, and a joint prayer was performed. The pilgrims left the holy cave and halted at Binakandi village for the night.

At Binakandi village, an incident took place that changed the course of the Zeliangrong political movement. Once the pilgrims reached Binakandi village, they dispersed towards their respective villages. Gaidinliu was housed in one of the villager's residence while Jadonang decided to spend the night in the *Kalum Kai/Kelumki*, the house of worship built under his direction. The next morning, i.e., 28 January, Gaidinliu learnt that Jadonang was seen weeping in the night and was very depressed. He seemed to have come to know about his fate which had been foretold by Tingwang after reading the notebook which he brought back from Bhubon cave. Gaidinliu was worried as there was already word out that the British authorities were on the lookout for Jadonang and Gaidinliu by falsely implicating them in a murder case of four missing Manipuri traders. The British were worried that the movement of Jadonang's Naga Raj will spread throughout the Naga Hills, hence the murder case presented them with a chance to arrest Jadonang and his follower Gaidinliu.

On the same day, a servant of Imtiaz Ali (an official interpreter of Lakhipur Thana, Cachar district, Assam) came to Binakandi village looking for Jadonang. By that time, Jadonang was quite well known in Barak Valley and the surrounding areas for his ability to cure sickness and various illnesses that dogged people of all communities.

The messenger gave the news that Imtiaz Ali's wife was not well, and Ali had requested Jadonang to come over to his house and treat her. Jadonang found the request to be quite normal and did not suspect anything as Imtiaz Ali was well known to him. However, Gaidinliu and the elders of Binakandi warned Jadonang to not accept the request as the situation had changed. The police and the CID were resorting to various means to arrest Jadonang and, moreover, it was odd that Imtiaz Ali himself did not come to fetch Jadonang. At this Jadonang simply dismissed their concern and said, 'Don't bother, I know Ali very well.' He downed a few gulps of *zaodui* (rice beer) and left with the messenger. It was later reported that Jadonang was taken to Ali's house via a different route and the messenger led him to the police station instead. The police party was waiting for him in a vehicle and Jadonang was immediately arrested and taken to Silchar Jail.

The next day, Gaidinliu disguised herself in a simple attire without any traditional jewellery or other paraphernalia and went to meet Jadonang in Silchar Jail on the pretext of bringing him some food. When she met him, she found Jadonang was angry at Ali's betrayal and shared his anxiety about the fate of the movement.

Gaidinliu advised him to be strong and stick to the truth till the end. She assured him that she would continue the Zeliangrong movement of both religious reformation and political protest along with all their supporters. She even suggested that if the police asked about the purpose of their visit to Bhubon cave, he should simply tell them that he went to worship the Almighty as was done since time immemorial. And if he has committed a crime for worshipping his God, they can arrest him as he was ready to bear any consequences as deemed fit.

This brave and daring act of Gaidinliu who risked being arrested by going in disguise to meet Jadonang also won the hearts and support of the followers. They were now ready to be led by her. It was said that during her journey back to her village, she was stopped multiple times at police checkpoints for verification. She escaped on each occasion with her quick thinking and presence of mind. Once she luckily wriggled out of a tight spot by telling the police party that Gaidinliu has just gone ahead of them and that they were also going back to the village of Longkao. The meeting between Gaidinliu and Jadonang was probably the last between the two pioneers, as soon after his arrest, he was taken to Imphal and charged with the murder of the Manipuri traders.

After the arrest of Jadonang by C. Gimson, deputy commisioner of Cachar, Assam, he was handed over to J.C. Higgins, the political agent of Manipur. The government decided to make a demonstration march of an Assam Rifles column from Jirighat to Longkao to Tamenglong and then to Imphal. It was during this march on 13 March 1931, that young Gaidinliu came to the notice of Political Agent J.C. Higgins, SDO S.J. Duncan and Major Bulfield of the 4th Assam Rifles. Gaidinliu escaped into the Zeilad Lake Forest area accompanied by 40 youths, including some girls. She went into hiding waiting for the outcome of the trial of Jadonang at Imphal. She knew the truth and always insisted that Jadonang was innocent of murder and was not present at the scene of the crime. After the trial and unfortunate execution of Jadonang on 29 August 1931, Gaidinliu took up the cudgels for the people in revolt. Prof. Gangmumei Kamei[9] writes,

> The real revolt occurred after the martyrdom of Jadonang. Gaidinliu, the charismatic, spiritual and political successor of Jadonang was the leader of the rebellion. The revolt was a violent protest against

9 Kamei, *A History of the Zeliangrong Nagas.*

> British Imperialism and a logical consequence of the ideology and strategy of Jadonang, which would have taken shape but for the sudden, short and unexpected British clampdown on the protagonist of the 'Makam Gwangdi' or 'Naga Raj'. The arrest, trial and execution of Jadonang stunned his followers with fear and anxiety. His village, his own villagers disowned him. Jadonang's role was the preparatory phase and real action came during the phase of Gaidinliu, his brilliant and determined disciple. Success or failure, she did not care. Fight she must; she was determined to put the master's ideology into practice.

It was obvious that Jadonang was the pioneer of the Zeliangrong movement. He had successfully brought about reforms in Zeliangrong religion and, in the process, engineered a massive social movement involving all sections of the social strata and all the sub-tribes of the Zeliangrong community, the Rongmei, the Liangmei, the Zemei and the Puimei of Manipur state, North Cachar Hills and Naga Hills of the province of Assam. Such an electrifying phenomena of a tribal movement touching all aspects of social, religious, aesthetic and political life of a scattered Naga community had not been witnessed in the hills of North East India. Hence the continued legacy of Jadonang through the rebellion of Gaidinliu and her men was perceived as a grave threat and danger to the rule of the British. They were determined to put down the rebellion at any cost.

Though the British authorities launched a massive search operation to find and arrest Gaidinliu, she reached her village safely and soon news of her escape spread like wildfire and only added to the growing myth and stories about her special power which Tingkao Ragwang bestowed on her to lead her people. It was time to lead her people alone against the mighty colonial power and fight for her *Makam Gwangdi* or self-rule by her own people.[10]

10 The above narrations of the early enigmatic life of Rani Gaidinliu have been drawn from the writings of and conversations with many resource persons like Pautanzan Newme of Haflong, former general secretary of Zeliangrong Heraka Association (ZHA), Ramkui Wanbe Newmei of Lodiram, Haflong and president of ZHA, Chaoba Kamson, general secretary of Tingkao Ragwang Chapriak (TRC), Abuan Kamei, former PS to Rani Gaidinliu, and Prof. Gangmumei Kamei. The contribution of the author has been to place the accounts in a logical sequence for the easy understanding of the readers.

THE REBELLION
COLONIAL PHASE

After Jadonang's execution, Gaidinliu took up the leadership of the movement for social justice and independence. The British had let loose a reign of terror in the hills. They imposed collective fines on the rebel villages and all guns were confiscated. The British rule was arbitrary and oppressive. Gaidinliu told her followers, 'We are a free people. The white men should not rule over us. We will not pay house tax to the government. We will not obey their unjust laws like forced labour and compulsory porter subscription.' The response of the British government was very heavy handed. It passed laws for arbitrary arrests of people who were Gaidinliu's sympathisers and imposed heavy fines on villages giving shelter to the movement.

Thus the socio-religious reform movement of Jadonang and Gaidinliu was forced to transform itself into a political one due to the oppressive rule of the

British in their area of influence. Initially the movement had only social and religious aims. Socially, it aimed at the integration of the three main kindred tribes (Zemei, Liangmei, Rongmei) known as the Zeliangrongs. They wanted to preserve the traditional Naga culture and way of life and were against any alien religion overwhelming them. Gaidinliu soon refined the religious movement into a movement called the 'Heraka' which means pure. But the political reality of the oppressive rule by alien colonisers forced them to take up the cudgel for freedom, partly inspired by the raging call of Mahatma Gandhi for India's independence.

Gaidinliu's political agenda was inspired by Jadonang's political vision, *Makam Gwangdi* or self-rule. Many writers have speculated that Jadonang had earlier come to know of Gandhi's movement and incorporated it in his idea of *Makam Gwangdi* but it was Gaidinliu who used the name of the father of the nation in her political propaganda. She told her followers about the agitation launched by the Congress under the leadership of Gandhi. The timing was just right as the vacuum left by Jadonang needed to be filled after his untimely death; hence people looked towards the leadership of Gaidinliu. They believed in what she said and, in their love and reverence for her, they elevated her to the stature of a goddess bestowed with special powers. It was because of this overwhelming support of her followers that the British authorities and many writers following them, out of ignorance, opined that she installed herself as a goddess, which again was far from the truth.

After the execution of Jadonang, the whole affected areas comprising the present Manipur west district, present southern Nagaland and North Cachar Hills of Assam were alight with rebellion. Gaidinliu went underground to direct the rebellion. The British government was greatly alarmed at the unprecedented uprising under the leadership of the 'surly girl' of 17. However it was not a consequence of mob action of every 'crook and gangster' as Ursula Graham Bower thought, nor of 'ruffians', as Stephen Fuchs writes, nor was Gaidinliu 'the hub of a money-spinning God racket'.[1] These descriptions of Gaidinliu were rather unfortunately used by her political opponents to discredit and tarnish her reputation in her later years. In fact, her movement was a well-organised and popular political rebellion. Her people donated generously for the cause

1 Ursula Graham Bower, *Naga Path*, p. 46; Stephen Fuchs, *Rebellion Prophet*, p. 151.

and a large number of fighting men volunteered for the rebellion against the British authorities of Manipur and the Naga Hills. For her many followers, Gaidinliu was the only hope for their freedom.

The British government decided to suppress the rebellion and capture Gaidinliu, the hunt for whom was, in the words of Bower, 'Something almost comparable to the hunt for Prince Charlie.'[2] This was because the British government apprehended a grave danger to their rule in the NEFA[3] region if the spirit of defiance of such a movement were allowed to continue for long. Bower writes that the bulk of the Zemi (Zeliangrong) was with her. To make matters worse, the Zeliangrong country, according to Bower, was a maze of game trails, field tracks, paths, caves, deep forests and ravines. Every settlement had its own private pathways, its back entrance revealed to none including its secret hideouts. It was said that the abetting villages signalled and sent coded messages to each other by beacons and smokes and warned of

2 A term usually used based on the legendary hunt for the Scottish Prince, Bonnie Prince Charlie (real name, Charles Edward Stuart), who led an unsuccessful Jacobite rebellion to overthrow the Hanoverian 'usurper' George in 1745.

3 North East Frontier Areas (NEFA). During British rule, most of the north-east Indian region inhabited by the tribals was demarcated as NEFA for administrative purposes.

the movement of troops and patrols. In fact, Gaidinliu seemed to appear and disappear like a ghost.

Against this backdrop, the Assam Governor-in-Council ordered that the operations against Gaidinliu were to be centralised under the direct control of J.P. Mills, the deputy commissioner of Naga Hills, who could use the men of the 3rd and 4th Assam Rifles; the SDO of North Cachar Hills and the officers of Manipur state were to assist him. This was how serious the British authorities were about Gaidinliu's rebellion. Now troops were sent out to all three districts; outposts were established at strategic points; search parties were sent out for Gaidinliu; her photos were widely circulated throughout the three districts. In fact, it was said that all girls having the name of Gaidinliu or similar names were interrogated and the harassment meted out to them was so harsh that many girls who had the same name changed their names to avoid harassment. Even Gaidinliu had to adopt the name of 'Dilenliu' to avoid being noticed even by a slip of the tongue. Mr Harvey, the then president of the Manipur State Darbar, offered a reward of Rs 200 for the arrest of Gaidinliu; this amount was subsequently raised to Rs 500, a princely sum in those days, and any village giving information about her in the area was promised a remission of ten years' taxes. But the government did not fully comprehend the impact and hold the movement had on the people. The call for freedom from the suppression of the British held out more promise than a mere remission of taxes. In fact, every man and woman in the region was a sympathiser.

Gaidinliu went into hiding in the North Cachar Hills, and Masang of Kepelo, her agent and one of her most trusted followers, did his best to keep her whereabouts and movements a complete secret. It was reported that Masang was a very capable commander who had a vast network of spies in all the important villages and towns. Their methods were to utilise the myth and the aura surrounding Gaidinliu and her soldiers to employ deception in order to trick the British. Gaidinliu would come and go like a ghost, rumoured to be dressed in white and escorted by girls; people would whisper that her presence was felt only in spirit, and the maze of connections that they created in the villages concealed her movements. A network of tunnels, back entrances and secret hideouts made her inconspicuous to the British but very visible to the people. Their confidence and faith in her went from strength to strength. Rumours of her exploits—turning bullets into water and foiling assailants by her magic (*kiantau*)—spread like wildfire.

The local authorities became positively desperate and tried everything including conspiracies hatched to even get her married! In the game to arrest her, she was approached with a marriage proposal by one Lambu (a local official/record keeper) named Abungshon. Gaidinliu was said to have hoodwinked him and escaped along with her *Riphen* or rebel warriors. Meanwhile the Manipur government of those times meted out severe punishments to the supporters of the rebellion. Several villages were burnt down as a consequence.

The Battle at Hangrum

The sepoys of the Assam Rifles had an encounter with the rebels in North Cachar Hills on 16 February 1932. Long and difficult operations by the mighty colonial authorities followed in their attempt to capture the young rebel leader. On 18 March 1932, a large force of Zeliangrong Nagas attacked the Assam Rifles outpost at Hangrum in broad daylight. The rebels fought bravely even though they were not very well armed as they were using mostly traditional *dao*s and spears with very few crude guns, hence no match for the modern rifles of the defenders.

The outpost opened fire which caused some casualties among the rebels who quickly retreated preventing a massacre. Six Assam Rifles soldiers were killed and eight Zemei warriors were shot dead. The Assam Rifles contingent were surprised by how well the rebels fought. They found the rebels to be highly motivated and skilled fighters who fought fiercely and but for their inferior arms and weapons, would have come out victorious. The attack was led bravely by Heungchang Zemi. Gaidinliu seems to have trained and inspired them well to lead such a daring raid, even inflicting damages and loss of lives on the battled-hardened Assam Rifles.

Gaidinliu's primitive *dao*-and-spear-armed Zemei warriors were no match for the Assam Rifles. But the tribal warriors were inspired soldiers who believed in the power of their leader, the blessed Gaidinliu who would protect them and lead them to victory. The warriors were mostly from Hangrum village with reinforcement from the Bopungwemi village. Gaidinliu told her warriors that all the bullets of the Assam Rifles would turn into water. Ursula Graham Bower writes sarcastically,

> It would be really interesting to know now whether she really believed in her own powers. At any rate,

> Hangrum (who could, had they been attacking rationally, have crept up at night through the dead ground and rushed the post easily), made a massed charge in daylight, down the only slope on which the sepoys commanded a field of fire. It will always be a mystery to those who know the place why three times the number were not killed. When the first volley, fired over their heads, brought them howling on encouraged, the next was sent into them at thirty yards range; with the obvious consequences.[4]

Bower was right in a way; it did not make sense to attack during broad daylight, that too, when the Assam Rifles sepoys occupied the vantage points. But the supporters of Gaidinliu believed that her blessings reduced the casualties despite the disadvantages faced by her brave warriors. The warriors comprising of mainly the Zemei supporters were led under the leadership of Heungchang Zemei. According to Jukambe Jeme, as told to Dwijendra Nath Sharma of the *Amrita Bazar Patrika* of 3 June 1987, the following were killed in the battle of Hangrum:

---

4 Ursula Graham Bower, *Naga Path* (Guwahati/Delhi: Spectrum Publications, 2003), p. 47.

1. Nramgraing Zemei
2. Namkabuing
3. Paudi Rangbe
4. Keruingjing
5. Lungsangding
6. Zimbuing
7. Ketewangbe
8. Rameteung

The leader of the attackers Heungchang Zemei received a bullet injury on his right knee. He survived the injury and died in 1985.

The hunt for Gaidinliu and her followers by the British was well described by Bower who wrote,

> To make things worst she was often present in spirit, and panting sepoys, sent out the best information found Nagas dancing solemnly before the empty throne. To crown it all, she was on the principle of 'darkest below the lamp' concealed for three months within the sight of the outpost at Hangrum. The village sent out to worship her everyday and when she left she told Hangrum that they could attack the outpost without getting hurt.

> She had, she said, bewitched the sepoy's rifles.
> Their bullets were water, they would not kill.[5]

As retaliation, the British authorities ordered the burning down of Bopungwemi village in the Naga Hills and innocent villagers were tortured. Gaidinliu and her group of rebels moved eastward and reached the edge of the Angami country. Her influence also reached the Maram Nagas of Mao area in northern Manipur. Even in Kohima, the headquarter of the Naga Hills, her sympathisers were many. The 'Gaidinliu water', which was said to have been blessed by her and which many believed had the power to cure common diseases, was reported to have sold for high prices in many Angami villages. J.P. Mills, the deputy commissioner, who reported earlier that the 'real danger of the movement is the spirit of defiance now aboard', had to act promptly to prevent any alliance between Gaidinliu and the powerful Naga village of Khonoma which staged a great uprising in 1879. It was also reported that Gaidinliu's followers were fomenting possible alliance with other Naga tribes like the Maos, Marams and Angamis. It was believed that many sympathisers were working as spies

5 Ibid.

for Gaidinliu at Kohima itself to check the movement of the Assam Rifles detachment stationed there.

The British government felt that there was an urgent need to put down the rebellion as it had the potential to foment further troubles for them if it was allowed to fester. Therefore, it was determined to crush the rebellion by all means. They feared that if the spirit of defiance spread to other tribal communities it might lead to uncontrollable rebellions. From their records, it was clear that they mocked and at the same time baulked at the very idea of the unlettered tribals rising up against the yoke of colonial power. This can be seen in the Assam government's report to the Government of India on 20 February 1932:

> Jadonang who, claim to be their Messiah King was responsible for the trouble that occurred last year, was convicted and hanged for murder, and it was thought that the unrest would then cease. Unfortunately, the woman Gaidinliu who was associated with Jadonang, as a priestess, reappeared among those people apparently with some man impersonating Jadonang, who was said to have come to life again. The arrival of

> the Deputy Commissioner (J.P. Mills) with the detachment of Assam Rifles at Henima led to the flight of the woman and her party, but she had already established the belief that the 'Messiah King' was among them. And that it was to the Kukis, has for the moment been dispelled by the presence of Assam Rifles but it will clearly take time to undo the mischief which has been cleverly engineered by the imposters. Every attempt is being made to capture the woman, Gaidinliu who had escaped apparently with a large escort into the North Cachar hills. Detachment of Assam Rifles are pursuing her and her party.'[6]

The news of the operation against Gaidinliu was spread far and wide in the Naga-inhabited area, while in Manipur it was completely blacked out. The Assam Rifles as an intimidation method burnt down several villages. The S.D.O., Northwest, C.S. Booth was involved in the atrocities inflicted on the Zeliangrong youth while pretending to be in pursuit of Gaidinliu. This reflected not only the sick mentality of the officers but also the

6 Asoso Yunou, *The Naga Struggle Against the British under Jadonang and Rani Gaidinliu* (Kohima: self published, 1984), pp 90-1.

frustration they felt at their own inability to arrest a 'mere' woman/girl who continued to elude their dragnet. On the other hand, there was sympathy for Gaidinliu, and spies were at work in Kohima, Imphal, Haflong and Tamenglong. Gaidinliu's 'water', as mentioned earlier, was said to have sold for Rs 10 per bottle even in Kohima where there was a great demand because of the supposedly legendary healing powers. Bower said that the water was from the pond of Thinge and a scam was afoot perhaps without the knowledge of Gaidinliu. As harsh a critic as she was, Bower admitted that the racket was clearly run by some unscrupulous elements out to take advantage of the gullible people without the obvious knowledge of the main protagonist.

After the attack on Hangrum, Gaidinliu went into hiding in the Naga Hills again. And the search continued. The 'hunt for Prince Charlie' continued, as Nari Rustomji[7] writes.

> An elaborate saga had meanwhile grown around her name to the extent that she had become a supernatural being and could elude her captors

7 N.K. Rustomji, *Enchanted Frontiers* (Delhi: Oxford University Press, 1971), pp 102-6.

> through her magical power, appearing in several places at the same time. The troops were baffled, as she was rumoured always to be in a dozen places at one time.

The elaborate plan to surround herself with mystical aura may have been a deliberate effort on the part of her intelligent followers like Masang to befool the authorities. It was obvious that she had no magical powers. The popular support of the people and the secret paths saved her.

J.P. Mills, the operational-in-charge, wrote of the Zeliangrong rebellion led by the elusive Gaidinliu on 1 January 1932. According to Mills, the aims of the movement are based on the old belief that a Naga king will one day arise. Jadonang who was believed still to be present in spirit was held to be that king who will reign with Gaidinliu. The belief was summed up in the slogan, 'The day of the Naga is coming.' This saying was obviously translated to Mills from the sayings of Jadonang: '*Makaamei roi Guangtupuni*'.

Mills interpreted that this slogan necessarily involves the disappearance of the British rule and the subjugation of the Kukis. He wrote,

> Against us, there is no bitterness at all, but the Kukis are hated. Latecomers into the hills, and living scattered among Naga villages they are regarded as interlopers and the feeling against them is kept alive by stories (in which there is a considerable stratum of truth) of atrocities committed by them on the Nagas and of adherents as more immediate ones of health and wealth. It is believed that by obeying her order and doing ceremonies in her honour, sickness will be banished and herbs and crops will flourish. The immediate aim of Gaidinliu and the medium is undoubtedly notoriety. Fame and offering are pleasant things.[8]

Clearly the British were trying to portray Gaidinliu's action as her desire for fame without realising that it was the people's support which had kept them at bay from arresting her. This note also revealed the not-so-subtle attempt at divide and rule by the British officials taking advantage of the Kuki-Naga saga.

In another note, J.P. Mills further dwelled on the implication of the movement. He wrote,

8 J.P. Mills, *A Note on Gaidinliu's Movement,* June 6, 1932, Kohima.

> The real danger of the movement is the spirit of defiance now aboard. Nagas who are ordinarily truthful and friendly have been taught that officers are to be lied to as deprival of information. These lessons will not be quickly forgotten. The capture of Gaidinliu will not end the agitation. There is a warrant of murder out against her and she can be dealt with when caught. She will be succeeded by one or more 'medium', and to be a medium is not offence under any law. Yet they will continue to keep people in a state of constant excitement, and Nagas will continue to be set over against the Government and Kukis. The result from administrative point of view will be serious. Once she is in our hands, we just aim at gradually suppressing the movement by punishment, persuasion and personal influences. This will be our task.[9]

Against this operational strategy of the British government, Gaidinliu organised her forces. As

9 Assam Secretariat, Political, June 1933, Note 58-315, quoted in Robert Reid, *History of the Frontier Areas Bordering on Assam* (Shillong, 1942; Reprint, Spectrum Publication, Guwahati/Delhi).

mentioned earlier in the chapter, Masang of Kepelo was the commander of her army. Masang was a staunch follower who believed in the immortality or divinity of Gaidinliu. He was the in-charge of her movement and kept the whereabouts of Gaidinliu a complete secret. Gaidinliu employed a number of spies to report on the movement of government troops. She also tried to build up alliance with the Maos, Marams and the Angamis of Khonoma. There was general sympathy for the mystic rebel fighter girl but there was no concrete support forthcoming. Khonoma stood beside her, but not with any military help.

After the Hangrum incident, Gaidinliu with a few adherents moved into the Naga Hills. The people had been tortured, their villages burnt, nine in all. A collective fine of Rs 2920 and 29 guns were imposed. Gaidinliu planned to take one last stand at Pulomi (Poilwa) in her fight against the British forces.

Gaidinliu at Pulomi (Poilwa) Village

In early October 1932, Gaidinliu moved into Pulomi (Poilwa) village where she and her supporters were welcomed by the people. Poilwa was chosen as the general headquarter of the movement because of its strategic location (it was only around 30 km from Kohima), its abundant resources like surplus food, and most importantly the people of Poilwa were opposed to the British rule and had a long history of resisting the British's forays into the Naga Hills since 1832. Gaidinliu's army was reorganised and regenerated under the command of Masang, her loyal follower. Under her instructions, they started the construction of an amazing wooden fortress after the pattern of Assam Rifles palisade at Hangrum. Gaidinliu told her followers that the next two months would be a crucial period; either she or the British would win. She was prepared to make one last trial of strength between the Assam Rifles and her army. It was an ambitious plan; the fortress when completed would accommodate four thousand warriors and would be a formidable one for any army. It was also at Poilwa that Gaidinliu is said to have met Dr Haralu, the medical pioneer from Kohima, and his family. Though Dr Haralu's family supported Gaidinliu's movement, especially her daughter Miss Neichunliu Haralu, who later became the Indian Ambassador to Panama and her brother T. Haralu, who later on joined the Indian Frontier Administrative Service, Dr Haralu himself was strongly opposed to Gaidinliu's ideology. In the meantime, J.P. Mills got an intelligence report about the construction of the fort and immediately dispatched a strong force of Assam Rifles under the command of Captain MacDonald accompanied by Hari Blah, the Extra Assistant Commissioner (EAC). It was believed that Dr Haralu and one Ishingbe had a hand in the so called 'intelligence source' that J.P. Mills got on the whereabouts of Gaidinliu. Both Dr Haralu and Ishingbe were the minority voice of the village who felt that the villagers were being misled by the Rani and that her ill-equipped army had no chance against the mighty British. To hoodwink the spies she was known to have in Kohima, Mills ordered a diversion by sending a false expedition in the wrong direction in a blaze of glory giving it a grand send-off at Kohima. The real troops under Captain MacDonald left at dusk, unnoticed, on a thirty miles night track.

During the author's field visit to Poilwa, the village elders led by Shri I. Daniel Zeliang recounted that Rani Gaidinliu was hosted by Mrs Heulamhing of Ngalui clan and listed some important individuals who were in charge of defence, supply, musical band, women's group and spiritual guidance. It was a well-organised set up and the strategy was to attack the Kohima outpost of the British after the harvest season in late November when more *Riphens* from other surrounding Zeliangrong villages would join them.

Meanwhile the fortress though under construction was not yet ready and the rebels had not taken any precautionary measures against such an attack. Captain MacDonald made a surprise attack at dawn on 17 October 1932. The rebels were completely taken by surprise and could not offer any effective resistance. According to an insider version, the breach of the incomplete fortress was possible because Dr Haralu accompanied the Assam Rifles forces. Moreover, the villager recounted that Dr Haralu's own elder brother, Ikwamheung, was on guard on that fateful day and he was unable to shoot his muzzle rifle at his own brother. In the ensuing melee and confusion, the Assam Rifles troops breached the fortified gate and managed to surprise the rebels. They surrendered to prevent any massacre and harassment to the villagers and Gaidinliu was arrested from a house. She was taken to Kohima and brought to Imphal for trial. Mr Higgins, the political agent, sentenced her to life imprisonment. She spent 14 years in British colonial prisons, the first year at Gauhati, six years in Shillong, three years in Aizawl, Mizo Hills and four years in Tura, Garo Hills.

Many of her followers were also arrested and imprisoned, though pockets of resistance erupted through rebels proclaiming similar agendas against the government such as refusal to pay house tax, etc. The government took some harsh measures as precaution by arresting the remnants of the rebels, particularly those alleged to have been involved in the revenge killing of a Kuki family at Lakema, rumoured to be responsible for the tip-off that lead to Gaidinliu's arrest. In due course of time, most of the accused were arrested but pockets of resistance continued to surface in the form of 'prophets' claiming to be reincarnations of or in communication with Jadonang and Gaidinliu. For instance, one Gomhei appeared claiming divine powers along with a girl, Areliu, and toured villages curing diseases and preaching the coming of the Zeliangrong empire and their own apotheosis.

Despite the government's repressive measures, the movement continued in one form or the other. A Liangmei priest, Haideo of Pabram, a medium in the words of J.P. Mills, was the first prophet to have claimed the possession of power to heal the sick and perform ceremonies with Jadonang and Gaidinliu. It appears that Gaidinliu was in touch with some of her trusted followers. Haideo claimed that he was blessed by God to usher in the kingdom that Jadonang promised and asked the people to not pay taxes to the government. He preached the reformed religion as enunciated by Gaidinliu in the villages of Tamenglong, North Cachar and Naga Hills. The government of Assam came to know of his activities and it was decided to suppress him. Haideo fled to Henima and ultimately was arrested by the Assam Rifles in May 1934 and imprisoned. He was regarded as an active and devoted lieutenant of Gaidinliu.

The Zemei village of Bopungwemi which was burnt down by the Assam Rifles was the strongest base of Gaidinliu's movement. Ramjo is believed to have led a raiding party at Lakema as revenge for the arrest of Gaidinliu and killed some Kuki villagers. The Kukis were alleged to have informed the authorities about the whereabouts of the rebels. Ramjo was the most heroic of all the leaders in the Naga Hills. He was a staunch advisor of Haideo after his arrest and, in fact, he also managed to elude arrest by the Assam Rifles for two years, moving from village to village, thus keeping the rebellion alive. He asked the people to not pay taxes to the government and was finally arrested in 1934. Though Ramjo was charged with the murder of the Kukis at Lakema, the government could not prove any of the charges. Having failed to prove the charges against him, the British authorities detained him as a state prisoner under the Regulation Act of 1818 which allowed preventive detention by the state. Ramjo died in prison.

Dikeo was another brave warrior whom the government was trying to arrest for his involvement in Gaidinliu's rebellion and subsequently Ramjo's movement. Dikeo was also arrested along with Ramjo in 1934 but escaped heroically from the custody of Assam Rifles at Henima and absconded for many years. He continued to keep the flames of Gaidinliu's rebellion alive but was shot dead by the Assam Rifles in November 1940.

Gaidinliu's followers continued to be inspired by her and the movement carried on in a few pockets in the Zeliangrong country. Leaders like Masang, Ghumeo, and Dikheo managed to escape from the authorities but, without the main inspirational leadership of Gaidinliu, they could not restore the movement to its earlier intensity. According to Bower, the overall poverty and sufferings permeating the Zeliangrong country and their desire for a better condition of life also led to a strong belief in these millenarian 'prophets'. In fact, Bower, who was working in the Zeliangrong area around this time as an anthropologist, recounts an experience in which she is presumed to be Gaidinliu's incarnation, in a kind of apotheosis. Bower[10] records her conversation with Gaidinliu's disciple and righthand man Masang, then a part of her entourage:

> But before Gaidinliu was arrested she had told Masang and the rest that even if she was caught it would not matter; the Government would imprison only her simulacrum and her real and divine self would be safe elsewhere, to return in the course of time in such a shape that her enemies would never know her and only the faithful could recognise her. Masang had not forgotten. After all those years he was still looking for her reincarnation.
>
> I didn't know it at the time, but he found it in me.

This despite the fact that Bower was very critical of Gaidinliu, viewing her uprising as a means of exploiting

10 Bower, *Naga Path.*

the economic malaise in the region with its promise of future wealth and prosperity from the divine source. Their only commonality was their gender, their assertiveness, and their independence and autonomous lifestyles. But she admitted that Gaidinliu could not have found a better or more loyal follower than Masang who strongly stood by her till his last breath.

Pandit Jawaharlal Nehru and 'Rani' Gaidinliu

Around December 1937, Jawaharlal Nehru while touring undivided Assam as president of the Indian National Congress, as it was his wont, threw himself into the affairs of the state. Nehru realised that Assam was confronted with a number of complicated problems like tea gardens labourers, immigration, inner line permit system, opium dealings, poverty, the excluded area and partially excluded area of the hill tribes of Assam, etc. To understand the problems besetting the state of Assam, he started meeting all the stakeholders, representatives from different communities, tribal groups and various splinter groups. It was during such interactions with some Congressmen from Cachar in the Surma valley that Nehru first heard about the heroic deeds and struggles of Jadonang and Gaidinliu. He was very impressed by the fact that Gaidinliu was recognised by her Naga people, especially the Zeliangrong tribes, as their saviour and leader. A visionary freedom fighter and a romantic writer, Jawaharlal Nehru was greatly impressed by the exploits of Gaidinliu and was shocked that a young Naga girl should suffer so much at the hands of the British.

While Nehru was in Sylhet in December 1937, he wrote,

> In Sylhet also, many Nagas from the surrounding hills came to visit me with greetings and gifts. From them and others, I heard a story which India ought to know and cherish. It was a story of a young woman of their tribe belonging to the Kabui clan in the Naga Hills. She was of the priestly class and she had the unique opportunity to receive her education in a mission school [this was probably misinformed to Nehru as Gaidinliu was unlettered], where she reached the ninth or tenth class. Gaidinliu was her name and she was about nineteen, six years ago when the civil disobedience movement blazed over the length and breadth of India, news of Gandhi and the Congress reached her in her hill abode and found an echo in her heart. She dreamt of freedom

for her people and the ending of all restrictions they suffered from, she raised the banner of independence and called her people to rally around it. Perhaps, she thought rather prematurely, that the British Empire was fading out. But that Empire still functioned effectively and aggressively and it took vengeance on her and her people. Many villages were burnt and destroyed and this heroic girl was captured and sentenced to transportation for life. And now she lies in some prison in Assam, wasting her bright young womanhood in dark cells and solitude. Six years she has been there. What torment and suppression of spirit they have brought to her, who in the prime of her youth dared to challenge an Empire! She can roam no more in her hill country through the forest glades, or sing in the fresh crisp air of the mountains. This wild thing sits cabined in darkness with a few yards of space in the daytime, yearning her heart in desolation and confinement. And India does not even know of this brave child of her hills, with pride. A day will come when India will remember her and cherish her, and bring her out of her prison cell.[11]

11 Yunou, *The Naga Struggle against the British*.

Nehru wanted to know whether the provincial government led by the Congress party could do something to release Gaidinliu but was frustrated to find that under the Government of India Act, 1935, the Excluded Areas were not under the jurisdiction of the provincial ministry of Assam. Even questions about Gaidinliu were not allowed to be put up in the Assam assembly. Deeply affected by this development, Nehru wrote in his tour diary,

> Darkness had set in and my tour was approaching its end. We reached Habibganj late in the evening and after the meeting there, hurried on to Haistabganj to catch our train. The crescent moon hung over the horizon, with its silvery brightness gone and looking gloomy and yellow. I thought of the past twelve days with all their quick movement and crowds and enthusiasm, and it all seemed like a dream that was over. And I thought of Gaidinliu, the Rani, sitting in her prison cell. What thoughts were hers, what regrets, what dreams?[12]

12 Ibid.

Nehru later went on to Shillong, the capital of Assam, and met her in Shillong Jail. During their warm and sentimental meeting, Nehru was moved by her story and praised her for fighting the mighty British Empire in her Naga Hills. Then he hailed her, for the first time, as the queen of her people, 'Rani' of the Nagas, and promised to use all his influence to get her released from the British jail. He further said that in case his efforts failed, India was going to gain independence very soon from the British, and in that case she will automatically be freed. Gaidinliu was deeply touched by the words of Nehru and she humbly accepted the symbolic title of Rani prefixing her name Gaidinliu, and since then she came to be widely known as 'Rani Gaidinliu'. In an article published in *Hindustan Times* on 18 December 1937, Nehru described her as 'Rani' and this title stuck to her ever since.

Nehru's visit to Assam in 1937 and his emotional meeting with Gaidinliu in Shillong instilled in him a tremendous interest about the other hill people of Assam like the Nagas, Garos, Khasis, Jaintias, Lushais, Abors, Miris, Mikirs, etc., as they were all living in impoverished conditions in the Indian border areas, totally isolated and neglected. He tried to help Gaidinliu by insisting that the Congress government of British India put in their best possible efforts to secure her release from jail. However, their attempts were unsuccessful as the Congress government had no political or legal powers to deal directly with the princely state of Manipur and the Excluded Area of the Naga Hills.

Pandit Nehru's Correspondence with Lady Nancy Astor

Nehru was determined to set Rani Gaidinliu free at all costs. In June 1938, Pandit Nehru appealed to the influential Conservative member of the British parliament, Lady Nancy Astor (1879-1964) to help the Naga freedom fighter, Rani Gaidinliu. Accordingly, she and some other members of the British parliament did their best by taking up the Rani's case with the British government of India.

But the Assam government was firmly opposed to her release. The local officers in Manipur state and Naga Hills district of Assam were fully convinced that the movement of Jadonang and Rani Gaidinliu would be revived at any opportune time with the return of Gaidinliu to the hills, and her old followers would strive together with her for their cause once more. Therefore they felt that there was every possibility of recurrence of the sinister trouble and disturbance throughout the Naga inhabited areas in Manipur, the Naga Hills, North Cachar and Mikir Hills. Consequently the request of the members of the British parliament was turned down by the secretary of state for India by stating that Gaidinliu was a serious criminal convicted for murder and rebellion, and her release would be an act of mockery of justice, inviting a law-and-order problem in the area, detrimental to imperial interest. The secretary of state also stressed the fact that the matter of Gaidinliu's sentence is one for the Crown representative and the question relates to the internal affairs of the Manipur state and not to British territory. The above facts were mentioned in Lady Astor's letter dated 10 May 1939 to Nehru (see Appendix-II).

Nehru also wrote to the premier (chief) minister of Assam, Gopinath Bordoloi, the Assamese Congress leader, and entrusted him to find out something more about the facts of her case. Accordingly, Bordoloi made an enquiry using his official channels, however limited it may have been, as the case was under the purview of the Manipur government and the British governor of Assam. With the available information, Bordoloi had written to Nehru on 24 March 1939 that according to the reports received by him, Rani Gaidinliu proclaimed herself as the queen of the Nagas after the execution of Jadonang, the leader of the rebellion and a convicted criminal, and this has not gone down well with the British government.

Nehru again wrote to the premier of Assam on 18 April 1939 from Allahabad that the facts provided to him were interesting but he would like to read the official version of her case as the version provided by the India Office in London seemed a curious one. He wanted to check the facts further. Once again, on 22 May 1939, the premier of Assam, Gopinath Bordoloi, sent to Nehru all the important censored documents of the official version of the movement of Jadonang and Rani Gaidinliu without much comment on the matter. Nehru also wrote a letter to Lady Astor thanking her for her efforts on the matter (see Appendix-III). He remarked in the letter that

> … the girl must be an unusually interesting person if she is still supposed to be 'a potent source of danger' to the peace of Manipur state and the province of Assam. I should have thought that the peace of Manipur State and the province of Assam had a very insecure foundation if it rested on a girl in her twenties to be kept in prison indefinitely.

There was also support from unexpected quarters for the release of Gaidinliu from imprisonment. In 1938, Hijam Irabot Singh, the president of Akhil Manipur Mahasabha, got a resolution passed demanding Gaidinliu's release from Shillong Jail. The government of Manipur and Assam firmly rejected the demand. In response to the growing demand for her release, the president of Manipur State Durbar, T.A. Sharpe, issued an offensive statement in retaliation. He declared that Gaidinliu should not be called a Rani, or Queen of the Nagas, as she is at best, a heinous political rebel. She was, in fact, according to Sharpe, in reality a sorceress, addicted to the cult of human sacrifice. Sharpe further pointed out that the title of 'Rani' was given to her by Pandit Jawaharlal Nehru who was totally ignorant on this subject and this was 'to be expected from a political agitator speaking without serious preparation'. In response, Nehru dedicated an editorial on Manipur state in the *National Herald* on 10 March 1940 where he wrote,

> Manipur State is little known in rest of India except for the Manipuri Dance which deservedly grows but we also think of this State in connection with Rani Gaidinliu, the brave Naga girl who still

> lies in prison somewhere in Assam because of what she is alleged to have done some years ago. When the demand for the release of this girl was made, a minister of this state who is an English official issued an offensive statement, on which we had occasion to comment.

He went on to highlight the brief history of the region and condemned the action of the British government in Manipur and critiqued the British policy of the border areas.

Nehru's attempt to release Rani Gaidinliu and the Manipur Mahasabha's demand for her release were ignored by the British political agent and the Maharaja of Manipur. The colonial authorities backed by the ruling circles condemned the Zeliangrong leaders, Jadonang and Rani Gaidinliu. Even a school textbook condemned the rebellion. The Zeliangrong government employees in Manipur and Kohima, under pressure from the colonial employers, were forced to condemn the rebellion, though the common people did not agree with these condemnations.

By now the name of Rani Gaidinliu was ubiquitous in the region and her sympathisers also started calling her 'Rani' as a form of protest against the colonisers. Meanwhile, Rani Gaidinliu heard of all these events taking place in her land. She was waiting and praying for freedom within the four walls of her prison cell. While at Gauhati Jail, Gaidinliu undertook a fast unto death which many followers narrated was inspired by Gandhiji for her release. It was said that she fasted for 31 days till she was force fed by the authorities. However, by then the news of her fast had spread like wildfire and reached even Pandit Nehru.

With the Second World War at the doorstep with the bombing of Imphal and Kohima by the Japanese, the British authorities did not want to take any chances. She was taken to Shillong Jail and then to Aijal (Aizawl) in the Lushai Hills district of Assam. After this Gaidinliu was again shifted to Tura Jail in the Garo Hills district of Assam. She was not released till India got her independence in 1947, that too after the personal intervention of the first prime minister of independent India, Jawaharlal Nehru himself. That is another saga to be told in the next chapter.

THE REBELLION
POST-COLONIAL PHASE

Release of Rani Gaidinliu

Rani Gaidinliu was kept in Gauhati Jail for one year after the pronouncement of the life imprisonment sentence at Imphal in the Court of the Political Agent. Young Gaidinliu was barely 18 years old then. She did not know the local language, found Gauhati hot and humid, and she did not have suitable clothing either. She felt crushed, but her belief in God kept up her hope that she would be free one day despite the life imprisonment sentence. On her request, she was transferred to Shillong Jail after one year. In Shillong, she spent six years. From her later accounts it is apparent that she was treated well by the other Khasi prison mates. She could also establish contact with some of the tribesmen of the Naga Hills and North Cachar Hills. Khonoma men, and even Mokokchung Naga *dobhasis*, out of love, met her and gave her presents.[1]

1 Kamei, *A History of the Zeliangrong Nagas*, p. 182.

As narrated earlier, Pandit Nehru heard of her and later met her in Shillong Jail. She learnt to drape the all-white Assamese sari, learnt Khasi and the Assamese languages. She became quite popular inside the jail. Her fight with the British became well known. From Shillong she was transferred to Aijal (Aizawl) Jail for another six years. There she learnt the Mizo language. At the time of the Japanese invasion, Rani Gaidinliu was transferred again to Tura Jail. Nehru ensured that she was a popular prisoner by applying repeated pressure for her release and describing her as 'Rani'.

After the Second World War, one Mrs Phillips Jones of Oxfordshire, England made a frantic attempt to locate Rani Gaidinliu whose fight against the British was discussed in the British House of Commons. She approached the secretary of state for India to get her released. The India Office in London referred the matter to the viceroy and ultimately to the governor of Assam. Nari Rustomji, advisor to the governor of Assam, refused to take a sympathetic view of Rani Gaidinliu.

In 1947 when Jawaharlal Nehru became the interim prime minister of India, the local state government of Assam was under pressure to release Rani Gaidinliu. This led to her eventual release from Tura Jail. Mrs

Phillips Jones's persistence and the intervention by the prime minister did the job, overruling the bureaucrats in Shillong and Imphal. One condition was put forward by the government of Manipur: she would not be allowed to return to her native state Manipur for five years. Hence she was settled at a Naga village of Yimrap near Mokokchung along with her brother Khiusinnang in erstwhile Naga Hills district of Assam with many restrictions imposed on her movement. During her stay in Yimrap village in Mokokchung area, her brother married a Chang Naga girl and settled there. She was granted a section of armed guards from the Nagaland police, a government accommodation and freedom fighter pension of Rs 15 per month from the Manipur and Nagaland governments. She made some lifelong friends among the local Aos and Chang elders, especially Mr Sashimeren Aier, a young student leader who took up her case. An eyewitness account by Captain Maharaj Priya Brata Singh, the younger brother of Maharaj Bodhichandra Singh, who was in the 1st Bn. Assam Regiment and met her at Yimrap is as follows,

> ... many years later, when I was in the army, I had the occasion to tour then Naga Hills. Near

> Mokokchung, one of my porters told me that at Yimrap village a 'Kacha Nagani' was staying. The word struck me and I wanted to meet her. Myself, the porter and my orderly, one Rupunanleng went to the house of the 'Nagani'. A slim and tall lady, all in white, perhaps a sari, asked me what I wanted. I spoke in Manipuri, and she also knew Manipuri, I said, 'Who are you?' She replied, 'Gaidinliu'. I suddenly remembered the girl whom the British tried to arrest and put in jail long ago. I asked her what she was doing. She told me that the Government put her in Yimrap and did not allow her to return to Manipur. She was given a monthly pension of Rs 15/; she was with her brother. But she was living in that village as a native.[2]

Priya Brata Singh also recounted his meeting with Gaidinliu's mother in her native village of Longkao (also known as Nungkao). He writes,

> Still later when I became the Chief Minister of Manipur, I happened to visit Nungkao village in

2 Maharajakumar Priya Brata Singh, in his 'Foreword' to Kamei, *Jadonang: A Mystic Naga Rebel*.

> Tamenglong. It was an orderly Pagin, a Kuki who with a certain fear told me that Nungkao was village of Rani Gaidinliu. The whole village took interest in me. I was accompanied by Rashid Ali, Commandant of 4th Assam Rifles. Bob Khathing, the Hill Minister had gone ahead for shooting monkeys, so Rashid and myself went to Nungkao. I met the mother of Gaidinliu who wept and requested me to return her daughter. I told her that I had met Gaidinliu long ago in Yimrap. The villagers showed me the site of the temple built by Gaidinliu long ago. I saw the charred remains of the wooden posts.

After five years she was allowed to enter Manipur in 1952 when restriction on her movement was lifted. She also met Prime Minister Nehru during his visit to Imphal the same year. She settled down in Tamenglong headquarter in quest of a peaceful life. She met Prime Minister Nehru and her daughter Indira Gandhi in 1958 in Delhi.

Rani Gaidinliu continued to work for the social and economic development of her people in the area of Manipur, Nagaland and North Cachar Hills of

Assam. She worked tirelessly for the unity and ethnic consolidation of the cognate tribes namely, Zemei, Liangmei and Rongmei including Puimei or Inpuimei, into one ethnic group known as the Zeliangrong. This evolution and consolidation of the kindred tribes had started when Gaidinliu was in prison. In 1947, at the initiative of Namgaheing Iheilung, a policeman of Assam police, and K. Kakhangai of Kakhulong, Imphal formed the Zeliangrong Union by performing the *Chuksu Garoumei* ceremony or 'traditional oath-taking ceremony' to stay together in unity come what may, based on common history, culture and way of life. The idea of a common Zeliangrong association took root in earlier bodies such as Kabui Chingsang (1925), Kabui Samiti (1935), and Kabui Naga Association (1947). Though the Zeliangrong elites started the process of consolidation of the kindred tribes into a common platform, it was the culmination and reflection of the vision of Jadonang and Gaidinliu. According to Prof. Gangmumei Kamei,[3] the creation of the Zeliangrong fraternity was the greatest achievement of the Zeliangrong people in the 20th century. The feeling of oneness had persisted despite the differences in political perception and objectives,

3 Kamei, *A History of the Zeliangrong Nagas*, p. 184.

the mainstream Indian democratic process, ethnic nationalism or ethnic regionalism of the Zeliangrong people. Religious diversity (Christianity and indigenous religious faith), inter-cognate group self-identity assertion, lack of common language and administration are not necessarily barriers to the evolution of the common Zeliangrong identity.

After the departure of the British, the political development in the Zeliangrong country was conditioned by the political processes unfolding in the Naga Hills district (now Nagaland), state of Manipur and North Cachar Hills district of Assam. The Zeliangrong people were drawn into the Naga independence movement initiated by the Naga National Council (NNC) started by Zappuh Phizo. They participated in Phizo's political activities and joined the Naga rebellion. In Manipur, the Zeliangrong people participated in the democratic process of the state initiated by the Maharaja and the liberal leaders who were influenced by mainstream Indian nationalism, though there were regional and Meitei nationalists who believed in the autonomy and regionalism of the state. The North Cachar Hills did not have a separate political identity like the Eastern India Tribal Union, based in Shillong, where leaders like Rev. Nichols Roy participated in the Constitution drafting process and pleaded for autonomy of the hill areas of Assam culminating in the Sixth Schedule of the Constitution. Manipur's participation in the Indian Republic after her merger was dominated by 23 years of Central rule, people's dissatisfaction and movement for statehood. There was also an extension of the Naga insurgency in the Zeliangrong area which can be explained as a reaction against Indian rule represented by the unpopular governments of Manipur and Assam. The Zeliangrong people also extensively pushed for 'Homeland movement' under the leadership of Rani Gaidinliu. According to Prof. Kamei, this was a reflection of the three trends of the Zeliangrong political perceptions: participation in the Indian political process was necessary for social and economic development; the homeland was necessary for the strengthening of the Zeliangrong identity and Zeliangrong regionalism; and participation in Naga insurgency was the identification of the Zeliangrong with the greater pan-Naga identity. Moreover, it can be argued that it was the Zeliangrong people who started the 'Naga Raj' movement under Jadonang and Gaidinliu.

The Naga Nationalist Movement Under NNC

In Nagaland, the Naga National Council (NNC) completely dominated the political scene from 1947 onwards. Post-Independence, the NNC did not accept the Constitution of India being drafted by the Constituent Assembly. The advisory committee on autonomy for the hill tribes of Assam appointed by the Constituent Assembly persuaded A.Z. Phizo, president of the NNC, to accept the autonomy based on the nine-point agreement which was ultimately written into the Sixth Schedule of the Indian Constitution. However, the moderates were overwhelmed by the extremist Naga nationalists in the NNC and they took a firm stand of complete independence for the Nagas. The NNC organised a 'Naga Voluntary Plebiscite' on 16 May 1951. The people put their thumb impressions on the declaration of the NNC that the Nagas were an independent nation and they wanted to remain so.

The NNC's talks with the governor-general of India, C. Rajagopalachari, and later with Prime Minister Nehru did not produce any result. The open standoff came to the fore during Nehru's visit to Kohima in 1953, accompanied by the then Burmese (Myanmar) Prime Minister U Nu, which was boycotted by the Nagas. A fierce conflict started between the Indian Army and the Naga Home Guards.

This was a result of the two different perceptions in post-Independent India. The Indian government's understanding was that after the British departure, the British-Indian provinces including Assam were automatically transferred to the dominion of India which became a republic in 1950. The NNC's point of view was that as per the memorandum to the Statutory Commission led by Sir John Simon in 1929, the Naga Hills/Naga Areas were 'Excluded Areas' which were not covered by the Assam Legislative Assembly under the Government of India Act 1935. They were convinced that Naga areas were not a part of the province of Assam and hence they declared independence. The NNC boycotted the 1st General Election and the Assam Legislative Assembly in 1952.

Naga People's Convention 1957-59

Meanwhile the moderate Zeliangrong political elements who wanted peace joined the Naga Peoples' Convention (NPC) which was formed in 1957 and proposed the formation of a union territory under the External Affairs Ministry, known as the Naga Hills Tuengsang Area

(NHTA). In 1960, as per the Delhi Agreement which was also known as the Nehru-Imkongliba Agreement, the Indian government agreed to constitute the state of Nagaland within the Indian Union. An interim body which was a pre-state assembly was formed and the state was inaugurated on 1 December 1963. During this phase of the movement for autonomy within India, the Zeliangrong leaders undertook prominent roles in the creation of the state of Nagaland.

Autonomous District Council in North Cachar Hills of Assam

The several demands for autonomy of the hill districts of Assam at the time of Independence were accommodated in the Sixth Schedule of the Indian Constitution. The United Mikirs and the North Cachar Hills District was given an Autonomous District Council. The Zemeis of North Cachar Hills who formed a minority participated both in the district council and the state assembly elections.

Political Development in the Naga Areas of Manipur Hills

The princely state of Manipur's journey towards democracy in Independent India was quite unlike that of the rest of the country. Prior to the departure of the British, the then king of Manipur, Maharaj Bodhchandra Singh, realising the democratic aspirations of the people of his kingdom made some important legislations. However, the Manipur State Constitution Act, 1947 which had a constitutional monarchy as its head and a right to choose the chief minister circumcised the democratic rights of the people.

Amidst the ensuing political turmoil, the Government of India decided to merge Manipur with India. The MLAs from the hills including the two Zeliangrong MLAs protested vehemently but to no avail. The decades following the merger were harrowing for the Zeliangrong people. In the absence of the people's representatives, almost all political activities ceased.

Rise of Naga Rebels, 1960 Onwards

The absence of democratic rights of the people post the merger of Manipur with India in 1949 and the insensitive bureaucratic rule made the Naga leaders question the wisdom of associating with the Indian state. The stage was set for a major standoff and in 1956 the Naga rebellion broke out. The Zeliangrong villages in the Manipur hills gave shelter to the rebels simply because they were their kinsmen. Meanwhile the Zeliangrong youth who were attracted towards the movement, joined as volunteers and became 'national workers'. Soon it became a community participation for the Naga cause. After this, the infrastructure consisting of the NNC, FGN (Federal Government of Nagaland) and the Naga Home Guards (as the Naga army was known) were set up in the Zeliangrong areas. Till 1959, the ill-equipped forces of the Naga army were able to defend their 'homeland' from the Indian Army.

Conflict with Rani Gaidinliu

The leaders of the merged Zeliangrong Union had a difference of opinion on the question of integration of the Naga-inhabited areas including the present Tamenglong district into the future Naga national state. To discuss and find a way out, a joint meeting of the NNC, FGN and the Zeliangrong leaders was held at Kaikao village in present Tamenglong district in 1960. The meeting was hardly democratic, the FGN leaders forcing the Zeliangrong leaders present to take some controversial resolutions. The first resolution was that a separate administrative province will be given to the Zeliangrong in the proposed Federal Government of

Nagaland. Secondly, the meeting also resolved to accept Christianity as the official religion of FGN in proposed sovereign Nagaland. These two points formed the bone of contention for the followers of Rani Gaidinliu's ideology and thinking. Gaidinliu wanted a separate administrative unit for the Zeliangrong within the Indian Union. Her fight for independence was from the exploitative colonial British rule, inspired as she was by Gandhi's call for freedom. In the course of her journey she had become friends with Nehru and other leaders from the Indian mainstream. She was convinced that the future of the Nagas and the Zeliangrong people lies in India. In short, she was a staunch Indian nationalist. The second point of contention directly hit at the heart of Gaidinliu's religious reform movement 'Heraka' which formed the basis of her philosophical thought. Hence to even remotely agree to the terms and conditions laid down by the protagonists of the Naga independent sovereign state did not appeal to Rani Gaidinliu and her followers.

The NNC in the early days took Rani Gaidinliu lightly and took a very patronising view of her movement. They even sent a *Tatar* (minister) ranked official to persuade her for a tie-up in 1954. In fact, a cock was even sacrificed in a traditional oath-taking ritual as a mark of goodwill at Longkao village. This incident was witnessed by Mrs Namkhonliu, wife of C.R. Zeliang, a retired Indian Trade Service officer when she was just a young girl forming part of the Rani's entourage. But the talks did not go well as Rani Gaidinliu was very clear in her stand. The NNC warned her of dire consequences if she did not fall in line with their thinking. She was ridiculed as a follower of Satan and paganism. The NNC leaders considered the demand for a separate 'Zeliangrong Administrative Unit' as a big obstacle to the Naga's sovereignty movement. Rani Gaidinliu's revival movement of Heraka was severely criticised by the church leaders who termed it 'Anti-Christian'. The NNC's digression towards religious intolerance could perhaps be attributed to the overzealous enthusiasm of being new converts. Perhaps a saner approach may have prevented the deep enmity and hostilities between the two influential Naga groups which led to loss of lives on both sides. Early differentiation between politics and religion could perhaps have averted the conflicts that were to beset the relationship between the two Naga entities, both aiming to take the Naga people out from the deep morass they found themselves in at that point of time in their history.

Rani Gaidinliu was persuaded by her supporters to go underground since they were worried about her safety. The hostile NNC had by then declared her persona non grata. Gaidinliu was again in the jungles of her own country in independent India and was forced to form her own army with 500 warriors to fight and defend against the hostilities of the NNC who was determined to finish her off politically and ideologically. For them it was a fight to destroy an obstacle seen as an irritant to their goal for complete sovereignty. For Gaidinliu and her followers, it was a fight for survival against the hegemonic design of the NNC. The Federal rebels made repeated attempts to win over the followers of the Rani in vain.

The NNC entrusted their generals, Gen. Hulang and Gen. Thiubam, both from the Zeliangrong community, to talk to Rani Gaidinliu and her party. A meeting was arranged on 4 February 1961 between the two groups where the Rani was represented by Brig. Irangding, her advisor Azai, and the deputy commissioner of her government, Gongtinghing. At this meeting General Hulang arrogantly suggested that Gaidinliu should go to Delhi to demand Naga Independence and surrender their arms and ammunitions to the NNC. She was also insulted by being called the worshipper of evil spirits.

The talks continued for two more days, on 5th and 6th February, but broke down when the two parties stuck to their respective stands. In anger, the NNC troops torched the Phaiginlua village and fierce hostilities broke out.

Gaidinliu reiterated that she was a freedom fighter for her people and she refused to have any further political negotiations or talks with the NNC after this. She was prepared for a violent struggle if necessary to defend her religious and cultural identity against anyone, however powerful they may be, whether they came in the form of the colonial British or a hegemonistic group like the NNC. Now the armed conflict turned into a religious conflict based on certain ideological differences which could have been avoided. Many people lost their lives as both sides carried out attacks in the Zeliangrong country and an atmosphere of intolerance and fear prevailed all around. Many leaders of the Zeliangrong Union appealed to both parties to stop the enmity since both parties belonged to the greater pan-Naga family. Zeliangrong Christian missionaries also sent peace missions to both parties urging them to stop hostilities and return to work as everything had come to a standstill in the countryside.

Intervention by the Government of India

Subodh Chandra Dev, an IAS officer and a former deputy commissioner of Kohima, writes[4] that sometime in 1965, while trying to collect ration and money from the Zeliangrong people, a group of Federal rebels sent to the Rani a specific proposal to merge her movement with that of the Federal regime. When the hostilities were at their peak, as narrated above, the fate of the proposal became evident as all the nine rebels of the FGN were believed to be done to death and rumours started spreading that the Rani had gorged on their blood. She was thought to be a witch, a blood-thirsty vampire, even a goddess, and rumours were flying thick and fast. But the fact of the matter was that two groups who were ideologically and politically polar opposites of each other were engaged in conflict and the ensuing struggles involved violence against each other. There were casualties on both sides and many lives were lost. The tragedy of the whole situation meant that brothers belonging to same tribes were now ready to kill each other. The effects of the resultant propagandas against each other can be felt to this day. Misconceptions about

---

4 S.C. Dev, 'The Mystic Rani' in *Nagaland: The Untold Story* (Kolkata: Mrs. Gouri Dev, 1988).

each other has resulted in distrust and hatred between two groups who share a common origin and heritage.

By then, the Government of India had heard about the activities of Rani Gaidinliu. The newly installed chief minister of Nagaland state (Nagaland by then had been granted statehood in 1962 under the Indian Union), Shilu Ao was directed to persuade Rani Gaidinliu to come out of hiding and work for the development of her people. Shilu Ao handpicked S.C. Dev, an IAS officer, then serving as additional deputy commissioner of Zunheboto sub-division, for the post of the deputy commissioner (DC) of Kohima district. The brief by Shilu Ao was that since the Christians and the non-Christian Nagas, as well as people of other political faiths were agitated about the macabre allegations against Gaidinliu, the new DC would have to resolve the problem by either bringing her overground or driving her away from Nagaland. To this end, the chief minister seemed to have a plan worked out to shift the people of five villages namely, Nsong, Njana, Ngalong, Nkio and Lalong. His reasoning was simple. These five villages were the followers of the Heraka religion or cult as alleged and they offered Gaidinliu shelter and protection. Shilu Ao hoped that if the inhabitants of these villages were shifted to some place like Heningkungla near Dimapur, Gaidinliu would be compelled to shift her base outside the state of Nagaland, possibly to Manipur, and thus be dislodged from her stronghold. She and her men would be deprived of their food and refuge and then forced to surrender. The chief minister had even got an amount of rupees one lakh sanctioned by the governor of Nagaland for the purpose of shifting and rehabilitation of the five villages. In other words, the new state government decided to act like a bully while dealing with a political uprising by their own Naga brethren. Many researchers on the subject see this as replacement of one hegemonic ruler by another in the seemingly democratic and secular republic of India.

Thus the new DC was given a choice to either persuade Rani Gaidinliu to come overground or to uproot the population of the five villages which seemed quite unethical and insensitive. S.C. Dev decided to pursue the first course of action. He kept his plan a secret as public feelings in Kohima had turned against the Rani. The government of Nagaland in all probability would not have agreed to this plan either as many people wanted Gaidinliu to be captured and killed, taken in by the false propaganda spread by the NNC supporters and even by church leaders. Luckily, the new DC did not subscribe to their views because he did not believe that she was a traitor to her people or the country. He writes that his faith in her was justified later when the Rani told him that she used to celebrate 13 August as Independence Day to champion her cause for a Zeliangrong district to be carved out of portions in Assam and Manipur, not to assert her claim for secession from the Indian Union as some erroneously chose to believe.

Dev set about matters by camping at Henima village and reaching out to Rani Gaidinliu. She sent feelers through messengers about his intention to meet her in person. Meanwhile, the plan to depopulate the five villages were simultaneously going on, and the construction of seven extension barracks at Heningkungla started, big enough to accommodate all the men, women and children of the selected five villages. This was a psychological move aimed at the villagers and the new DC hoped that it might eventually force them to persuade the Rani to meet him. Despite all efforts, there was no response from the Rani's side so Dev had to return to Kohima again.

However, the DC did not give up hope as all the reports from his field officials convinced him that the

Rani had compassion for her people. So Dev went to Henima again, determined to meet her, and sent yet another letter serving the Rani an ultimatum to choose between meeting him and shifting the villagers. He allowed her 15 days to think it over and let him know her decision.

Gaidinliu had good political acumen, and she seemed to understand the DC's intentions and the possible repercussion of her decision on her people. On the last day of the deadline, Gaidinliu sent her emissary with a message that the DC should not shift the villagers and should wait for more envoys from the Rani within three days to meet her. This was agreed to by Dev and he arranged to have a meeting with the Rani's emissaries on the appointed day. Three days later, Mr Heirangding, commander-in-chief of the Rani's army, appeared with ten of his boys with a huge quantity of local drinks and a leg of sambar deer. This showed their friendly intention and when they got down to brass tacks, they brought the message that the Rani was willing to meet the DC if he volunteered to go to her camp. Without disclosing its location, the C-in-C said that they would have to travel on foot for four days to reach her camp. This also shows that the years of being underground in her long struggles against the British and now the NNC had transformed Gaidinliu into a hardened and wily political negotiator.

The DC did not agree to the proposal straightaway; after all he was dealing with the legendary Rani Gaidinliu. However, after discussing the matter at length he was convinced that no foul play was intended. Eventually, a compromise was reached; it was decided that both parties would march for two days and that they will meet at a halfway point.

The DC returned to Kohima the next day and consulted the chief minister and the chief secretary and, for the first time, he revealed his hopes of persuading Rani Gaidinliu to surrender. Any other method, he argued, would only send the Rani out of Nagaland thus enabling her to continue her movement in some neighbouring state. It would merely transfer, not end the problem. It was a powerful argument to which Shilu Ao and the chief secretary reluctantly came around as they were concerned for the DC's safety. However, since there was no plan B or better alternatives to deal with the crisis at hand, they decided to go with the DC's plan.

Preparations were made and all precautions as far as practicable were taken and the DC returned to Henima with a strong police force, and then commenced their march towards Nsong jungle. It was a tough journey no doubt and halfway through the expedition, they suddenly found two men waiting for them. One was named Huthumbo, a tribal council member, and the other was a messenger sent by Rani Gaidinliu. The DC was expecting some encouraging news from the messenger but was disappointed to learn that she would not see the DC unless he left behind his escort. The DC then realised that his party had been under a close watch all through their arduous trek, and every detail about his party had reached the Rani's camp. The Rani was not taking any chances now.

Confused, the young DC sought advice from his colleagues about their next course of action. It took them only a few minutes of deliberation to come to the conclusion that the DC should not proceed further. The DC's party were paralysed with fear of a woman who was believed to have recently killed nine people and then feasted on their blood. Moreover, if something untoward should have happened to the DC, they feared that the government might not only finish the Rani but also annihilate the entire people in the area. But Dev decided to go on without the escort party. Several civilians including officials volunteered to accompany him. Ultimately, a party of ten was formed. They were now ten unarmed men without any protection banking on faith in the sincerity of their mission and their government's moral strength.

Tired and exhausted, the DC's party made their way up the forest-covered steep hillock which was the Rani's hideout where they noticed numerous bunkers spread over, well-planned, well-built and well-guarded. It was a strange place and Dev realised how difficult it would be for a strong force to overrun this hideout even by air strikes.

The Meeting with the Legend at Nsong

The last climb to Nsong was back breaking and at one stage it was like climbing a tree. When they finally reached Nsong in the late afternoon, they were given accommodation inside the village. The Rani's camp was nearby. The DC was called to meet her at her camp and with a palpitating heart he obeyed the summons. Unlike his imagination of a hideously ugly woman garbed in flaming red robes, with piercing eyes, the Rani turned out to be an elderly woman nearing her seventies, fair complexioned, about 5'3" with wrinkles on her face, clad in traditional Zeliangrong Naga dress, wearing jungle boots with garlands in her hands to greet the new visitors. They came face to face and Gaidinliu greeted the DC with '*Jai Hind*' but added in Bengali, '*Chalaki karberi na*' (no tricks please).

Dev was quite embarrassed when the Rani asked him, 'Were you not afraid of coming to my hideout?' He replied in a fumbling tone, 'Well, yes, a bit scared no doubt. I believed you, and I came to you as a son does to his mother.' The Rani later told Dev, 'I felt moved when you addressed me as mother. I do not believe anybody easily, as I have been befooled earlier. But somehow, I have a feeling that you are not going to befool me.' Dev described his experience as an unbelievable one and after this they talked for three days and three nights, Dev trying to convince the Rani of the purpose of their visit.

During the long negotiations and talks, the party avoided any reference to the tales of blood and gore attributed to her. But during one of the discussions, an unintentional reference enraged her, and in a red-hot mood she said that was how people were disgracing her, some defaming her for their own advantage. She added,

> I am a simple illiterate woman, I please no spirit and worship none except the Almighty God.

> Human blood is pious to me as to anybody else. My cause is simple and straight—the cause of my people—the Zeliangrong Nagas. I have fought for the independence of India along with Gandhi and Nehru. Our aim was to drive away the British. I am an Indian, whatever may happen; I will live in the union of India. For my people, I want no state, no country, but only a Zeliangrong district within the state of the Indian Union. At present, my Zeliangrong brothers and sisters belonging to the clans of Zeme, Liangmai and Rongmei are spread over in three different states—Nagaland, Manipur and Assam. I want to see them in one district. I do not claim to be the leader of a separate nation. However, I do enjoy the confidence of a section of the Indian nation and I want to see them living together in one district.[5]

During one of her discussions with Dev, the Rani clarified that she was not against Christianity or any other faith for that matter. But she did not approve of the overzealous converts to Christianity who had abandoned the rich cultural heritage of the Nagas and

5 Ibid.

were blindly copying the cheap aspects of Western life. She simply said, 'We are Nagas and should live like Nagas. We have beautiful folklores and folk songs, colourful dresses and culture. When we see these new converts copying the Western ways in a cheap manner, it pains me.' It was surprising for many in Dev's party when she said, 'If there's anybody who feels and thinks that he or she is Naga—I am the one. Also, if, there is anybody who feels and think that he or she is an Indian—it is me.' To her, the Nagas and the rest of the Indians were not separate. They were one forming the great Indian nation. Talking of their separation was nothing but madness for her. This showed that Gaidinliu was a staunch Indian nationalist.

After holding discussions for 21 long hours, intermittently interrupted for consulting with her followers, Gaidinliu seemed convinced of the sincerity of Subodh Chandra Dev's appeal. She agreed to go to Kohima with only a handful of her followers. However, she had certain conditions. She wanted to go to Delhi to meet Prime Minister Indira Gandhi with a rider that should the talks fail for any reason, the government should see to it that she quietly returned to her jungle hideout. The young IAS officer immediately agreed but he was asked to put it in writing in his own blood! (See Appendix-IV for the agreement.)

The joint party of Gaidinliu and the DC reached Kohima on 20 January 1966. Her presence in the town was electrifying. There was an endless flow of people curious to see her. Gaidinliu was not used to such crowds but she met people from all sections of society. It was obvious that the people who met her felt no danger or fear as she turned out to be a humble, simple and affectionate old lady. She seemed calm and composed with a glow on her face, a glow which can be described as an aura of someone who has attained spiritual nirvana. Looking at her and talking to her made one believe that the horrifying tales were lies—nothing but fabricated lies. At Kohima, she met many people including top officials and Chief Minister Shilu Ao who was requested to arrange the meeting with the prime minister. It was also said that some influential underground leaders wanted to meet her but she politely refused as it would have served no purpose. By then their views were poles apart.

The chief minister of Nagaland arranged a meeting between the Rani and Prime Minister Mrs Gandhi. S.C. Dev accompanied her to Delhi and also acted as an interpreter. Dev writes about the meeting in his book *Nagaland: The Untold Story*,

> The Prime Minister stood draped all over with the colourful Zeliang(rong) attire and jewellery presented to her by the Rani. Her native grace and charm combined with the colour and splendour of that exotic dress and ornament made the Prime Minister appear like a tribal queen, splendid but remote, different but of the land. Mrs Gandhi's magnetic personality seemed to cast a spell on the Rani and they warmly embraced each other.

Dev further writes that,

> With utmost consideration and sympathy the Prime Minister listened to her appeals, and assured her that she would do everything possible to develop the Zeliangrong area as quickly as possible. Regarding her demand for a separate district to be carved out of the Zeliangrong-majority areas in Manipur and Assam to provide a homeland for the Rani's people, the Prime Minister agreed to discuss it with other states at an appropriate time,

> ie after the insurgency in Nagaland was over. The Rani was happy that Mrs Gandhi talked to her and was impressed and gratified by the understanding, love and affection that had been shown to her.

But the problem was not yet over. About 300-400 of the Rani's followers were still lurking in the jungles. She persuaded them with her wisdom and authority and they ceremonially surrendered with their arms. Subsequently these men were absorbed in the Nagaland Armed Police. The Rani lived in Kohima from then onwards where she worked for the development of her people as a spiritual mentor and guide to her Heraka followers and worshippers of Tingkao Ragwang or Tingwang.

CONTINUED STRUGGLE FOR HER PEOPLE *THE ZELIANGRONG MOVEMENT*

Once Rani Gaidinliu came overground in 1966, she worked ceaselessly for the betterment of her people through democratic, non-violent and peaceful means. She became the centre of activities of the Zeliangrong people. Her first priority upon her return from meeting the prime minister, Mrs Gandhi, was to ensure that her armed followers numbering around 500 men and women were rehabilitated properly. She used her goodwill and authority to make them surrender with their arms to the government without any hiccups or misunderstanding. In fact, more than 300 of her followers were absorbed in the Nagaland Armed Police eventually. She used her hard-earned political stature to ensure a respectful rehabilitation package for her followers in a new political arrangement.

She wrote a letter to Mrs Gandhi for the consideration of the Zeliangrong problems with sympathy and wisdom in 1966. In 1968, the Rani and her delegation met the prime minister and submitted a memorandum on the Zeliangrong issues officially. Her political demand was the creation of a Zeliangrong Administrative Unit comprising the Zemei, Liangmei and Rongmei areas of Manipur, Nagaland and Assam. Though Mrs Gandhi promised economic development of her area and her people, Rani Gaidinliu remained committed to the original demand of a homeland for the Zeliangrong people which was the dream of her mentor Haipou Jadonang, who sacrificed his life during the freedom struggle against the British. During her trip to Delhi, she also met T.N. Kaul, the then foreign secretary, since the subject matter of Nagaland and NEFA region was being handled by the External Affairs Ministry. She also interacted with many prominent personages of Delhi like the diplomat B.K. Nehru who invited her to his residence for dinner. In all these meetings, she did not demand anything for herself and her consistent theme had always been the welfare of her people and their need for political space with social and economic development.

While she was settled at Kohima, the leaders of the Naga Integration Movement persuaded her to support their demand. General Kaito of the NNC met her on 6 October 1967 at Kohima to persuade her to join their forces together by leaving behind past misunderstandings. Though she sympathised with the other Naga political movements, she was completely committed to the demand for a Zeliangrong homeland.

Honoured by the Government of India and National Organisations

Rani Gaidinliu's stature as a freedom fighter of repute was growing nationally. While she was staying in Nagaland, she represented the state in national functions. She was made the president of the Nagaland Chapter of All India Freedom Fighters Associations. Her role in the freedom struggle against the British had become widely known. She was awarded the Tamrapatra in 1972 for her role in the freedom struggle. She was also actively involved by the government in the development of Zeliangrong areas, either for the creation of the district of Tamenglong in west Manipur or for the establishment of the Peren district in Nagaland, and for protection of the Zeliangrong people in North Cachar Hills or for granting of land for the settlement of the Rongmeis in Cachar, Assam. The Government of India honoured her by conferring on her the prestigious Padma Bhushan

Award in 1981. She became associated with several religious and cultural organisations. Rani Gaidinliu's name became synonymous with 'Heraka', the pure or reformed religion of the Zeliangrong. She became the preceptor, the philosopher, guide and driving force of the Heraka faith and formed the Zeliangrong Heraka Association with N.C. Zeliang as the founder president, an ex-MLA of Nagaland. She became closely associated with national, cultural and social organisations like the Kalyan Ashram, Vishwa Hindu Parishad and Vidya Bharti. She also became actively involved in the religious and cultural revivalism of the indigenous people of India.

The Zeliangrong People's Convention (ZPC)

The Zeliangrong People's Convention (ZPC) was established in 1980 at a conference held at Tamenglong, Manipur west district. Though Rani Gaidinliu did not attend the meet at Tamenglong, she sent her representatives to the conference and the house unanimously elected her as the first president of ZPC. The aim of the Zeliangrong People's Convention which popularly came to be known by its abbreviated name ZPC was the integration of all Zeliangrong areas into a single unit either as a district or a union territory or a state. The ZPC held three meetings in quick succession culminating in a final conference at Tamenglong on 30 November 1981 where it adopted the resolution for a Zeliangrong Homeland and unification of her people. The ZPC solemnly declared 30 November as the 'Zeliangrong Homeland demand Day'. (See Appendix-V.)

A series of democratic agitations were launched to pressurise the Government of India to grant the demand of the Zeliangrong people. Bandhs, hartals, dharnas, rallies, etc., were organised in all Zeliangrong-inhabited areas and also in the national capital, New Delhi. Despite the protests being non-violent, hundreds of volunteers were arrested and imprisoned. Supporters of the movement were fired upon and brutally assaulted by the security forces during the bandhs and strikes for Zeliangrong statehood.

Amidst the raging protests, Rani Gaidinliu and her ZPC delegation met Mrs Gandhi in New Delhi in October 1983 and submitted a memorandum of the Zeliangrong demands. She used her rapport with the prime minister to consider the aspirations of the Zeliangrong people. As a follow up to the meeting at Delhi, the Rani asked Mrs Gandhi for another meeting with her. The Prime Minister's Office (PMO) asked the Rani if she could come to Calcutta in December 1983 as the prime minister would be attending the Congress Party Plenary session there. The Rani and her ZPC delegates arrived in Calcutta on 28 December 1983. Abuan Kamei, the private secretary (PS) to the Rani, described the memorable meeting between the two women leaders, perhaps the two most fiery women of those times. It was said that when Mrs Gandhi reached the meeting venue, the Rani was already there waiting patiently for her and before the prime minister even settled down, she casually remarked that the Zeliangrong Homeland was not possible but she was ready to discuss the developmental package for the Zeliangrong areas. This remark upset Rani Gaidinliu and she got up from her seat and told the PM that she had struggled her entire life for a homeland for the Zeliangrong. In fact, that was the reason why she had fought for India's Independence along with Gandhiji and Mrs Gandhi's father, Jawaharlal Nehru. So she said that if the PM did not want to discuss the homeland demand, her effort of coming all the way to Calcutta was wasted, and she suddenly started walking out of the room. The Zeliangrong leaders which included Prof.

Gangmumei Kamei were shocked and the PM was left agape and speechless. Only Rani Gaidinliu could have got away with such an act. It was at this moment that Mrs Gandhi asked the delegates of the ZPC and the senior government officials to persuade the Rani to come back and she personally assured the Rani that the issue of Zeliangrong Homeland will be discussed. The meeting took place after this assurance and various issues were discussed including the homeland status and developmental package for the region. Abuan Kamei recalled that Prof. Gangmumei Kamei remarked that the meeting was the 'opening clash' between two great leaders. The PM sympathised with the Rani's demand but Mrs Gandhi's assassination in 1984 was a big setback for the movement as a whole. She continued the movement during the regime of Prime Minister Rajiv Gandhi who offered union territory status for the Zeliangrong areas and this was assured by Home Minister Buta Singh also, in a meeting with Rani Gaidinliu on 16 August 1986. Buta Singh assured the ZPC leaders that the Zeliangrong people would be integrated into a single union territory. However, the assurance was retracted by the Government of India and instead it offered the Central Development Authority (CDA), with the promise of setting up Zeliangrong Rifles, university and colleges, etc., in Zeliangrong areas. While negotiations were going on and before all these schemes could be finalised, Rajiv Gandhi lost power at the Centre which was once again a setback for the movement.

Rani Gaidinliu's anguish at the Government of India for not fulfilling its promise can be gauged in her speech at the ZPC Conference at Haflong, Assam on 15 October 1988,

> After many years of fierce struggles, I gave up violence as a means of political action in 1966 with the hope that justice will be done to my people by the Government of India. However, I am compelled to launch a peaceful political agitation as per the resolution of the ZPC. I have also informed personally about this decision to Prime Minister Rajiv Gandhi. I seek the cooperation of the liberal, patriotic and democratic forces in the country for fulfilling our long standing demand for Zeliangrong State within the Union of India. I believe India is a great Nation, magnanimous enough to accommodate the aspirations of a small ethnic group like the Zeliangrong people.

The ZPC continued to petition the successive governments at the Centre by submitting the memorandum to Prime Minister V.P. Singh in 1990 and Prime Minister Narasimha Rao in 1992. Though many meetings were held and agitations were carried out by the ZPC in the Zeliangrong areas, it came to a halt when the Kuki-Naga conflict occurred in late 1992. Then Rani Gaidinliu fell ill, left Kohima and stayed for two years in the village of Hejaichak in North Cachar Hills and one year in Hangrum village in Assam. There the elders from Longkao village came to see her and requested the villagers of Hangrum to allow 'Ranima' to spend the last days of her life in the village of her birth. Subsequently, she went to her native village of Longkao and after a brief illness, she passed away on 17 February 1993. With her passing, the Zeliangrong people lost an icon, mentor, guide and the greatest Zeliangrong leader of their times.

On her death, Prime Minister P.V. Narasimha Rao sent a condolence message: 'I am deeply aggrieved to learn of the sad demise of Rani Gaidinliu. Rani Gaidinliu was one of the most primeval freedom fighters of North East India.'

The governor of Manipur, Chintamani Panigrahi, who attended the funeral in the village of Longkao, described her as a great freedom fighter of India about whom he had read as a young student leader and whom he admired much in Manipur. She was mourned by thousands of her followers and admirers throughout the country.

Even in her death, she became a symbol of national integration. The Government of India honoured her further in later years by issuing a commemorative postal stamp in 1996. The Anthropological Survey of India conferred upon Rani Gaidinliu the Bhagwan Birsa Munda Puruskar with a citation and one lakh rupees in 1996 posthumously. The Department of Women and Child Development under the Ministry of HRD in the year 2000 instituted the Stree Shakti Award in her name along with five women leaders of India. A frigate class naval vessel was named *Rani Gaidinliu* by the Indian Navy in 2010. The birth centenary of Rani Gaidinliu was commemorated in 2015 in a year-long celebration by the Narendra Modi government in her honour and remembrance. Hence Rani Gaidinliu's contributions and sacrifices have been recognised by the Indian government but her original dream remains unfulfilled – the creation of a Zeliangrong Homeland.

THE ANCIENT ZELIANGRONG RELIGION AND THE RANI'S CONCEPT OF RELIGION

Ancient Zeliangrong Religion: The Concept and Philosophy

Prof. Gangmumei Kamei strongly reiterates that the Zeliangrong religion is an ancient religion, practised and preserved through oral traditions through the centuries. This religion is deeply rooted in the cultural heritage of the people. The Zeliangrong people understood their religion as a system of worship of God by men abiding by a certain code of spiritual, moral and social behaviour in dealing with God, men and society. The religion as such had no name initially. This led the earlier Western scholars, especially the anthropologists, to describe tribal religion as 'Animism' which means belief in spiritual beings, spirits, ghosts and demons. This was a mistaken notion. The fallacy of animism has been exposed to be an invalid concept. Terms like primal religion, primeval religion or primordial religion have been proposed by the scholars of philosophy and theology. Of these, the term 'primordial religion'[1] appears to be more accurate and an appropriate definition of the indigenous tribal religion including the Zeliangrong religion.

Primordial religion means a religion with a primordial existence. It has been existing since the beginning of time, and is ancient and eternal. The Zeliangrong religion is thus a primordial religion practised and followed by its people since creation. It is also polytheistic, a religion which worships many gods, goddesses, deities though it gives great primacy to the worship of the Supreme God, Tingkao Ragwang (in Rongmei) or Tingwang (in Zemei and Liangmei). Hence it has henotheistic features and believes in the Supreme God as the highest God out of the many gods.[2]

The Zeliangrong religion has the following tenets of a primordial religion:

1. Belief in the Supreme God Tingkao Ragwang or Tingwang who is the creator of the universe, gods,

---

1 Gangmumei Kamei, *Essays on Primordial Religion* (New Delhi: Akansha, 2006).

2 Gangmumei Kamei, *Tingkao Ragwang Chapriak: The Zeliangrong Primordial Religion* (Assam, Manipur & Nagaland: TRC Phom, 2005).

and men, who is benevolent and a protector of men. He is omniscient, omnipresent and omnipotent.

2. Belief in the existence of many gods and deities who are assigned by the heavenly God to look after different aspects of the world, nature and humans.
3. Belief in the concept of heaven, the abode of God, *Tingkao Ragwang Kai* or *Tingkao Kaidai*, and the life after death represented by the land of the death (*Taroilam*) where men's souls go after death.
4. Belief in the worship of the deities presiding over villages and places (*Shong* and *Bambu*) to act as the guardian deities of men in these villages.
5. Belief in the concept of ancestor worship (*Kairao Kalummei*) and in the concept of the rebirth of the human soul.
6. Worship of gods (*Ra Kalummei*) and propitiation of lower deities (*Ra Khaangmei*).
7. Belief in the concept of sin, which is known as *non* or *nuan*, as deviation from or violation of the religious, moral and social customs and norms, and retribution by God for the same.
8. Belief in the performance of rites of passage relating to birth, membership of social institutions, marriage and death (*Ringlon-Theilon*).

9. Belief in the redemption and salvation of the soul in heaven for good doers and retribution by the divine for bad doers.
10. Belief in the performance of festivals, ceremonies and rituals and other forms of religious and cultural expression of the worship of the divine.

These tenets clearly establish the Zeliangrong religion as a well-formulated, distinct religion with a well-defined theological foundation.

Myths of Creation: Universe, Gods and Men

According to *Encyclopaedia Britannica*, creation myths, also called cosmogonic myths, are philosophical and theological elaboration of the primal myth of creation within a religious community. The term myth here refers to the imaginative expression in narrative form of what is experienced or apprehended as basic reality. The term creation refers to the beginning of things, whether by the will and act of a transcendent being, by emanation from some ultimate source, or in any other way. The Zeliangrong community is an ancient community having its own cosmogony myth, philosophy and theological elaboration of the myth of creation which is quite interesting and unique.

According to myths and traditions of the Zeliangrong, Tingkao Ragwang willed to create the universe, gods, men and nature. He first created two deities, a primeval god and goddess, Didimpu and Didimpui (or Sudimpu and Sudimpui). As willed by Tingkao Ragwang, they created the sun, the moon, the stars, the water, the wind, fire, the earth, and seven layers of the sky.

Creation of Man

Tingkao Ragwang created two more deities—Dampapu and Dampapui—and directed that they create human beings. The couple in their attempt to create human beings, created a fish (*khagak*), a frog and a monkey. The Supreme God was not satisfied with these creations. Hence the fish was set free in the water, the frog was freed on land and the monkey was set free into the forests.

The two deities prayed to Tingkao Ragwang for advice. Tingkao Ragwang revealed to them His image to be adopted as a model or prototype of man. The story goes that the deities created a man and a woman out of the clay of an anthill. But they found that the created man and woman were lifeless and could not move their limbs. They ran out of ideas and felt helpless and again approached Tingkao Ragwang for His advice and help. It is said that the Supreme God appeared and breathed soul or life force on the head of the bodies and miraculously the man and woman became alive. Hence the Zeliangrong believed that the soul of a person is directly given by Tingkao Ragwang Himself to man.

Seven Brother Gods (*Ragwang Naren Chanei*)

Didimpu was made the lord of the earth and the king of the gods of the lower realm (Na-Ragwang) as per the wishes of Tingkao Ragwang. But he had no son, only daughters. He prayed to Tingkao Ragwang for a son. The Supreme God being a benevolent one granted the boon but with the condition that nobody should see him and his wife while making love. If anybody saw them in the act, the boon of the birth of the son would be transferred to that deity.

Didimpu had a sister deity named Charasinglangpui who was very fond of her brother, the king of kings. Her brother tried to send her away on different errands but, as fate would have it, one day Charasinglangpui entered the house of her brother to take a dried gourd water container and saw the couple while in bed.

Didimpu told his sister that as per the will of Tingkao Ragwang, she would conceive and give birth to eight sons. Charasinglangpui laid eight eggs which she put at the confluence of seven streams and returned home. The seven sons were hatched out of the eight eggs. The eighth egg could not hatch and remained as Dimei. The seven brothers returned to their mother who introduced them to their maternal uncle, the king of the gods of the earth. Didimpu offered them his daughters as brides and the youngest daughter was given to the youngest brother whom their mother favoured from the beginning.

Contest for Succession

The maternal uncle asked the seven brothers to take part in a contest for succession through feats of physical prowess like stone throwing, javelin throw, and wrestling between himself and his nephews. The eldest brother Bisnu was the strongest and most powerful but due to the machinations of their mother, the youngest brother outwitted the rest of the brothers and defeated his uncle. The mythical story also goes into the details of how the last contest in wrestling was unfairly won by the youngest son. It is said that the uncle defeated the six brothers but since the youngest son was married to his own daughter, the secret of defeating her father was shared with her husband. It was believed that the hair of Didimpu's wife was as hard and sharp as that of the porcupine and the hair was secretly thrown at the legs of the uncle who fell down on the ground and lost the contest. The youngest nephew tried to pull him up but Didimpu refused to get up and declared that the youngest brother would be his successor and the king of the gods of the world. And he himself would go down through the seven layers of the earth and become the king of earthquakes, Banglagwang.

Accordingly, the youngest brother succeeded to the office of Ragwang, the king of the gods of the earth, lower realm. He is known as Na-Ragwang, God of the lower realm, in contrast to Tingkao Ragwang, God of the Sky or Heaven. Bisnu, the eldest brother, was angry at this conspiratorial succession to the office of Ragwang. It was said that Bisnu protested and left the place by taking away with him the forest, birds and animals and even the seasons and took up residence at the holy cave in Bhubon Hills located in what is now eastern Cachar district in Assam. The world that was left behind for the youngest brother, the king, was a desolate and dreary place. After some time Ragwang tried to pacify his elder brother Bisnu by seeking the hands of the daughter of Bisnu in marriage for his own son. Bisnu was still annoyed. There was tension and conflict between the two powerful brothers and ultimately their uncle Banglagwang came out from the bowels of the earth and intervened for a settlement and ruled that:

1. The youngest brother would be Ragwang, the king of gods of the earth, as he had already given his word for the succession.
2. Bisnu, the eldest brother, would retain all powers wielded by him; and he would look after the affairs of nature, men, animals and deities. He would be the arbiter of men's relation with God.
3. The marriage of the daughter of Bisnu and the son of Ragwang was to be performed. But humankind should not follow this type of marriage of first parallel cousins.
4. Each of the brother gods were assigned powers and functions by their maternal uncle Banglagwang and given an area of jurisdiction as follows:

    - Ragwang, the king of the gods of the earth or lower realm (Na-Ragwang), took up residence at Mt. Koubru in what is now Manipur.

- Bisnu, the most powerful god on earth who looks after the affairs of men, nature and animals and communicates with men, took up abode at the holy cave of Bhubon Hills in what is now the Cachar district in Assam.
- Chonchai, who looks after the health of men and is said to be adverse to wine, resides at Mt. Kasuakbut in Taosang Khullen village in Tamenglong district of Manipur.
- Napsinmei (Laorang), the god in charge of food grains, took up abode at the peak of Naapsinmei hill (Phourungba) of Ganglon Namthan in the old Cachar road in Manipur.
- Charakilongmei, the god who keeps peace and wards off disturbances on earth, lives on a mountain peak of Bena village (Thonglang) at the western spur of Koubru mountain.
- Koklou, considered the *Peipou* or the owner of the office of the gods' court, resides at the peak over the Pouringlong village in the Koubru mountain in Manipur.
- Karangong, teaser of unruly youth and healer of man's sufferings from dizziness, is believed to reside at Puching (Khebaching) in Tamenglong.

- Dimei, the brother deity who did not hatch, remained in the water and earth. He is worshipped during the *Ralenloumei* ceremony.

The above account of the creation stories is mostly based on the Rongmei version. The Zemei and Liangmei version of creation follows the same basic storyline with some differences in the names of the protagonists with little divergence in the narrative plot of the stories and with a little fluctuating array of gods and goddesses. For instance, in the Zemei narrative, creation of man is attributed to Heratingrangpui (goddess) wherein she was forced upon by Maileng (Zemei are often known as children of Maileng), and then gives birth to all the creatures. However, in the Liangmei narrative like in Rongmei's, Charasinglangpui lays eight eggs by the river and gives birth to eight gods. The little difference in the narratives may be due to non-communication, inaccuracies in oral traditions, migrations, with the narrators themselves being located in different times and places. But what is important is that all three kindred group share a common cosmology. Similar strands in the stories prove their common origins and shared history.

There are also gods and deities in charge of the wind, fire, animals, weather, paddy, thunder and earthquake amongst the people. These gods are worshipped individually. Ragwang is offered sacrifices. Bisnu is widely worshipped in the Zeliangrong area, particularly during the pilgrimage to his holy cave. He is believed to be the transmitter of divine advice to the Zeliangrong people to worship Tingkao Ragwang. Napsinmei, Chonchai, Koklou, Charakilongmei are worshipped separately by villages as well as individuals. Karangong is worshipped for well-being and health purposes. The above concept and philosophy of the Zeliangrong religion was deeply rooted in its land, people and culture and it was under these circumstances that Gaidinliu and Jadonang rose like a phoenix in the Zeliangrong countryside to revive and reform the ancient religion of the great people.

Heraka

Rani Gaidinliu's commitment to her religious ideals and beliefs defined all her actions. Inspired early on by Haipou Jadonang's reform movement amongst the Zeliangrong, many followers of Gaidinliu were convinced that she was anointed by the Almighty, Tingkao Ragwang, to lead her people to salvation amidst the gloom and darkness prevalent in Zeliangrong society.

The Gaidinliu movement or the Heraka, as it came to be known in later years, spread in North Cachar Hills, Assam, from 1930s onwards as mentioned earlier. In the introduction to the *Zeliangrong Heraka Preacher Handbook* (1998), N.C. Zeliang, the past president of the Zeliangrong Heraka Association, says, 'Heraka literally means, in Zemei, "PURE". The Heraka religion is a pure or reformed religion of the Zeliangrong people comprising the three kindred tribes, the Zemei, Liangmei and Rongmei.' What Zeliang refers to is attributed to the Heraka adoption of one God, Tingwang/Tingkao Ragwang, and the subsequent ban on animal sacrifices. Thus the 'purity' is the metaphor for no blood sacrifices and the adoption of a single God.[3]

Another Zemei explanation for the meaning of Heraka is as follows: *Ka* means to fence, to obstruct, to avoid, to give up—all these words can be used in different contexts. *Hera* means 'small gods'. So all these *neube* (prohibitions in Zemei) and sacrifices associated with smaller gods must be fenced out, avoided, and only

3 Longkumer, 'Introduction' of *Poetry of Resistance – Heraka Movement*, p. 8.

Tingwang/Tingkao Ragwang must be worshipped. This is the meaning of Heraka.

So by fencing themselves in, by their acceptance of only one Supreme God, Tingwang, any threat is averted with the smaller gods, which is deeply embedded in the people's consciousness. On the other hand, the image of the fence that is protective retains much of the traditional understanding of purity and danger associated with any period of ritual. In this way, by giving up these gods, and the associated blood sacrifices, the Heraka are able to envisage a pure state, protected by the fence.

This is further clarified by Pautanzan Newme,[4] the former general secretary of the Heraka Association, when he explains that the Heraka movement can be seen as progressing through incremental changes and not wholesale rejection of the old ways by a completely new way. He describes the Heraka movement in four phases as listed below:

The first phase of teaching: Ranima told her followers to offer sacrifices to one God, Tingwang/Tingkao Ragwang. In this phase blood sacrifice was permitted.

---

4 Pautanzan Newme, 'Origin and Reformation of Heraka Religion' in *Heraka Golden Jubilee Souvenir* magazine (2001).

The second phase of teaching: This was introduced after 15 years. Ranima advised them while performing the ritual or 'puja' to cut with a *dao* (hacking knife) if it was big animal, and to use a stick (*nkiadang*) with smaller animals (like hen or cockerel) while holding the legs and to let the blood be shed. During this phase, the 'sacrificial ceremony was a bit diminished than the first phase'.

The third phase of teaching: In this stage, introduced after a further 10 years, Ranima instructed her followers that one should 'perform puja with the animal tied and its mouth stuffed with a rag and killed. But a chicken must be killed by hand, by twisting the neck, without oozing blood'. In this phase, the sacrifice of animals was further diminished.

The fourth phase of teaching: After about another five years the fourth phase was introduced. On 11 January 1990, at Kepelo village, North Cacher Hills,

> ... the preceptress (Ranima) vigorously declared and confessed before the general public that we have fully done the requirement of sacrificial oblation in puja. Now, influential sacrifices of animals in any puja are to be totally abolished.

> And we are free to perform puja with a clean mind and body at any specific time and day.

Pautanzan Newme further declares,

> … as advised by our beloved mother, Gaidinliu, we the Heraka people followed her path and lived happily free from trouble and worry. Abolishing of sacrifice brings about a strong sense of 'purity'. In freeing the people from sacrifices, Ranima alters the notion of sacrifice as gift. In other words, animal sacrifice constituted a gift to gods, but now, 'if anything is wrong with you, you may throw it upon me—I can affirmably bear things for your sake'.

This means that now, through her (Ranima), the people are free from the 'old' ways of appeasing the gods. This gives way to the 'new' – simply singing the psalms and praying with an empty hand. As the phases themselves suggest, the reform occurred over many years and was connected to many factors. Scholars like Arkotong Longkumer see the Heraka reform as a progression, an improvement on the traditional order.

Adopting One Supreme God, Tingwang/ Tingkao Ragwang

Rani Gaidinliu used the traditional understanding of Tingwang to preach that the Zeliangrong must reform their religion and make it clutter free by reposing their faith in a monotheistic Supreme God in line with other religions of the world. She actually derived the concept from the traditional understanding of the Zeliangrong religion by its people, simplified it and adopted a 'pure' way of worshipping God. She claimed that God has ordained her to spread this message of the reformation in the Bhubon cave and that all sacrifices and rituals for the lesser gods have to be cut down gradually and, ultimately, abolished.

According to N.C. Zeliang, the former president of the Zeliangrong Heraka Association, belief in the worship of one Supreme being, Tingwang/Tingkao Ragwang, is the introduction of the concept of monotheism or belief in one God in the Zeliangrong religion, which was traditionally a polytheistic religion, believing in many gods.[5] He strongly emphasised that Heraka is not a departure from the traditional Naga people but a rational improvement on it. This was

5 N.C. Zeliang, *Zeliangrong Heraka Preacher Handbook* (1998).

important because according to Rani Gaidinliu, the propitiation of many lesser gods through sacrifices of animals and rituals were becoming a big burden on the Zeliangrong people. Hence the adoption of Tingwang as the Supreme God was a rational progression for the Heraka, a pure reform religion.

The adoption of the monotheistic form of worship was also partly embraced by the Tingkao Ragwang Chapriak (TRC) which started organising themselves especially amongst the Rongmei group in the three states in the early 1990s. The TRC group had a more henotheistic approach as they accepted Tingkao Ragwang as their overarching Supreme God while not denying the space or existence of the lower deities as explained elsewhere in the book. The TRC movement was also inspired by the reform initiated by Jadonang and Gaidinliu and the movement has intrinsically adopted the teachings and reform processes of the two pioneers as their own.

The *Hingde* Book

When the British captured Gaidinliu in 1932, J.P. Mills confiscated her notebook which is now preserved in the Pitt Rivers Museum, Oxford, U.K. (please see the photos section). Sceptics like Mills dismissed the writing as nothing but meaningless scribbling, assuming that her 'literary power' gave her immense prestige. However, experts who have examined it have found it very cryptic though the meaning and the knowledge of the script is shrouded in mystery. One writer suggests that the script is the ancient Naga script founded by Jadonang; he apparently used it to compose hymns. Another writer claims that the script has been deciphered but it is still unsubstantiated. A section of the Heraka followers believed that Gaidinliu's notebook contains secret coded messages allegedly inscribed to help them achieve their goal of *Makam Gwangdi* or *Heguangram*, or 'land of freedom ruled by themselves'. Gaidinliu's own account says that it was received in the Bhubon cave and recalls that the walls of the cave were filled with writing. They transmitted an aura of the written form that she took down in detail. The notebooks are the only remnants of her writings.

According to scholars like A. Longkumer, the above narrative perhaps reflects the desire and need of the Heraka to have a holy book 'canonised' as the guide for everyday life on par with other religions of the world. Hence the reformers tried to codify the rules of living as given by Tingwang through Gaidinliu in the *Hingde* book. The *Hingde* book is didactic and peppered with insights, such as how to live according to Tingwang's will, or the codification of birth, marriage and death rituals, which become a 'sacred repository of the word of God'. *Hingde* literally means 'rules governing everyday life'. The etymological meaning of the term 'Hingde' is derived from the word 'Hede' which means 'to occlude'. 'Hing' means 'to be afraid of or to be followed' and 'De' means 'to occlude or a barrier'. Thus, *Hingde* means a reasonable restricted barrier which is to be followed or be afraid of.[6] The *Hingde* book tries to establish a connection between the present practice of the Heraka and that of the eternal religious practices. The Heraka followers believe in its existence since time immemorial. Most Heraka followers agree with the argument that if Muslims can have their Quran and Christians their Bible, both supposedly written to discipline their followers' lives through the teachings, why not the Heraka adherents? Hence, the Heraka is similarly attempting to systematise religious belief and practices. For example, the *Hingde* book speaks about eight steps that encapsulate 'Heraka Hingde'. They are as follows:

6 Widonlule Newme, trans., *Tingwang Hingde* (Zeliangrong Heraka Association, North East India, 2019).

1. Tingwang created the earth and will destroy again, but believe in Him and sing his praise and pray to him.
2. Respect your parents and elders and preserve the good Zeliangrong culture.
3. Have a disciplined mind and a clean body. *Heleuraube* (Selflessness) will make your image wonderful and you will become the son/daughter of Tingwang.
4. In all your speech and work your mind must be truthful. Search for knowledge and light but breed not jealousy and enmity.
5. Love all Tingwang's sons and daughters and search the way for happiness and peace.
6. Observe *Jalua* (full moon day).
7. Set up *Kelumki* (prayer house) and pray with an empty hand (i.e. stop animal sacrifice).
8. Have faith in rebirth.[7]
9. Haipei Gaidinliu is the harbinger of Tingwang and Her testimonies must never be manipulated.[8]

---

7 From *Tingwang Hingde*, 1991 (R. Newme).

8 This ninth step was seen only in the English edition of the *Hingde* book (2019), and may have been added later.

This codifying of rules according to Longkumer is an attempt to organise Heraka society under the rubric of *Hingde*. In fact, Longkumer noticed that people were encouraged, like the Baptist Christians, to talk about their faith and belief in order to project themselves as having a testimony—a transformative experience.[9] In other words, it gave the Heraka a sense of identity through the uniformity it espouses through the *Hingde*. The Heraka are adamant that they are the torchbearers of Zeliangrong tradition and by reforming they are merely establishing an original link with the past. The new *Hingde* replaced the old *Paupaise/Pupouchapriak Hingde*. Longkumer in the course of his fieldwork found that small gods associated with animal sacrifices have been eradicated to a large extent. The *Hingde* book has generously quoted the teachings of 'Haipei Rani Gaidinliu' who emphasised on giving up the worshipping of smaller deities and giving offerings to them. She recommended strongly that if Tingwang's name is chanted and the *Hingde* (law) is faithfully adopted, no evil can trouble or harm the believers. Rani Gaidinliu is quoted in the *Hingde* book saying a transient mind is harmful. She

9 Longkumer, *Poetry of Resistance*.

relates it with the incident that occurred during one of her visits to the holy cave of Bhubon Hills with Haipou Jadonang and their followers. When their followers were collecting droplets of the holy water (*Telaudui*), whoever kept running after collecting every droplet of the holy water from different spots thinking they might be able to collect more were in reality collecting less. But whoever, with one state of mind, remained patient and collected the droplets from one spot, were able to fill their pitcher. Likewise, a mystic/holy person could be easily recognised even through the simple act of collecting holy water. Rani Gaidinliu seems to be using this metaphor to send a message to the followers of Heraka to stick to the traditional Heraka religion and that only then will redemption be achieved.

The followers of Heraka believe that different generations require different practices, so each generation has a prescribed *Hingde* as per Tingwang's will. In order to reform the old practices, the establishment of *Kelumki* (prayer house) became necessary where prayers and teachings have to be a communal affair.

Growth of the *Kelumki* (House of Worship) as the Central Sacred Space

According to the *Tingwang Hingde*,[10] when Haipou Jadonang and Haipei Rani Gaidinliu went on pilgrimage to the holy Bhubon cave during the period between 1928 and 1931, Tingwang told them to build a *Kelumki* and worship there. Furthermore, Tingwang added, 'Hark! If you (Heraka folks) are to build a *Kelumki* then build it in like to my home.' In many ways the *Kelumki* resembles the entrance to the holy Bhubon cave, considered the abode of the Lord or Tingwang. It was told that the *Kelumki* can be designed and decorated depending upon one's capability keeping the basic structure unaltered. Hence a *Kelumki* can be built with thatch, tin or brick.

The *Kelumki*s were first built at Puilon (Jadonang's village), Longkao (Gaidinliu's village) and Binakandi (the village at the foothills of Bhubon Hills), and people started gathering and worshipping there. But due to various historical reasons narrated earlier, the British authorities destroyed these earliest *Kelumki*s. Moreover, the British prevented other Zeliangrong villages from setting up *Kelumki*s due to the political unrest that unfolded during the rebellions.

10 Ibid., p. 108.

With the establishment of the *Kelumki*, a sacred space was created for rituals and prayers. The *Kelumki* is separated from the rest of the village in the way it is planned, as well as physically treated and respected. It is the most 'sacred' ground for the Heraka and every Heraka village must have one. It is usually built at the highest point of the village. It is said that it is the exact copy of the first temple built by Jadonang and Ranima. It is also said that the exact structure appeared to Ranima in a dream. Every *Kelumki* must have a *naimik kakelum be bam* (literally, sunrise prayer place) outside facing the east. Facing the east is important as it is the direction of the Bhubon cave as well as sunrise. This is of great importance especially during the observance of *Jalua* (full moon ritual). In front of the *Kelumki* is the altar, centrally placed and elevated. One must climb three steps (symbolising life-death-life) to the altar, proceeding first with the right leg, then left and again right. The importance of the right and left is maintained in the *Kelumki* because it represents the balance between purity and impurity. Thus, the *Kelumki* is a sacred place in the Heraka world as all religious rituals and teachings are communally conducted here. By sacralising the *Kelumki* space, the Heraka makes the *Kelumki* the centre of the village replacing the old *hezoa* (similar to *daan bam* in Rongmei villages).

The *Tingwang Hingde*[11] further lays down ways and ethics of worshipping at the *Kelumki* as espoused by Rani Gaidinliu:

1. Kelumki is an immaculate abode. Thus one must visit Kelumki with clean body and mind. A devotee must keep his/her mouth clean and wash his face and should fast before prayer.
2. Inside Kelumki it is prohibited to wear footwear and cap and one should leave the head uncovered.
3. After entering Kelumki, devotees must face toward the Altar and stand by it and pray. While praying one must stand and keep his palms together.
4. Any person having ill health and wants to offer prayer can do so. One can pray for all good fortune and surrender all his worries onto Tingwang.
5. Flowers can be offered while praying as they are pure and it was evident that Tingwang is

11 Ibid., pp 109-10.

fond of flowers. In her lucid dream *(Mangdak)* Haipui Rani Gaidinliu saw varieties of beautiful flowers blooming luxuriously in the garden of Tingwang.

6. Even if the Kelumki is closed one can pray from the compound of Kelumki by facing towards the supposed chapel.

Thus the *Kelumki* became the centre of social and religious activities of the people. A place where people can meet fellow followers, thus providing them with a sense of belonging and identity. It also became a social space where similar opinions could be shared in relation with other competing ways of life and thinking. In the modern context, the *Kelumki* has become a new institution for socio-religious activities.

Similar importance is given to the *Kalum Kai* (house of worship) amongst the TRC followers. The *Kalum Kai*s were set up in various villages and settlements of the TRC followers in the three states of Manipur, Assam and Nagaland. According to the latest estimate, when the silver jubilee of the biggest *Kalum Kai* in Imphal was celebrated, there were 26 *Kalum Kai*s in Manipur, Assam and Nagaland.

All socio-religious and cultural activities of the TRC followers have started to revolve around the *Kalum Kai* and it has taken a firm root amongst the people.

Importance of *Zao* (Sacred Wine/Beer) in Heraka

The *zao* is a sacred wine/rice beer and its use forms an important part of the Zeliangrong tradition. The *zao* over the years has been used for many purposes. It has a medicinal purpose, helps in relaxation after a long tiring day in the fields, and is used during all ritual occasions. Once the liquid is filtered, the fermented rice is also used for many cures. It was used as a medicine in earlier times. People even believed that intoxication makes a person prone to 'divine communication', citing the example of Jadonang who took *zao* to go into a trance to communicate with God.

The *zao* is also used during performance of rites of passage like birth, marriage and death/funeral rituals. As in all tribal practices, as also for the Heraka, every public occasion is graced with *zao* and the lack of it symbolises the lack of hospitality. Sometimes its excessive use has led to other competing religions like Christianity in their various denominations drawing a line between those who consume alcohol and those who do not. Researchers like Longkumer have noticed that only the old Paupaise and Heraka will publicly drink *zao* at home or during festivals without really examining the double standards of other so-called modern religious groups. This has obviously invited derision from other religions, calling them '*zao jangmei*', meaning 'alcohol drinker' to refer to their religion. Perhaps if a survey is conducted across all religions, it will come to the conclusion that alcoholism is a social malaise inflicting all religious groups.

From an economic point of view, this unwillingness to give up the *zao* practice and its brewing and selling made sense for the manufacturers as it brought in monetary benefits. However, this issue of excessive drinking leading to drop-outs in education, unemployment, marital discords and other negative social impacts have forced the Heraka leaders to discourage the use of excessive *zao* as it is affecting the moral balance of the follower and hindering development of the society. This may perhaps be the result of the competing ideologies of the religious groups like the Baptists who encourage total prohibition of alcohol amongst their followers especially in the Naga Hills. But this is a problem afflicting all religious groups.

In Manipur its women activists known as *Meira Paibis* took up the issue and forced its government to prohibit alcohol totally in their state. Similarly, the Naga mothers and the church groups have strongly supported the total prohibition in the state of Nagaland. Keeping with the times, it may perhaps be prudent and practical for the Heraka to adopt the lesser use of *zao* in their ever-changing rules of life through their *Hingde* book for the future generations.

Heraka's Relationship with Christianity

A community does not exist in isolation. The Zeliangrong has to negotiate with the various 'boundaries', whether real or imagined, in the region they find themselves in. It is important to understand the relationship between the dominant religions such as Christianity and Hinduism and the Heraka/TRC, and how Rani Gaidinliu negotiated these relationships keeping her own religious reform movement in focus.

When the Christian missions first arrived in the Zeliangrong areas and many local people started converting, the missions emphasised the difference between Christianity and traditional Zeliangrong customs. Christianity became a distinct system with its particular form of worship, rituals, and its insistence on altering certain notions of traditional life. Scholars like Richard Eaton[12] cite the example of the Ao area. When the new converts were asked to observe a 'day of rest', it became highly controversial as it went against the rhythm and routine of Naga life that relied on communal participation for it to be efficacious. Similarly, among the Zeliangrong, new converts to Christianity were ousted from their villages and property confiscated leading to founding of new habitations and villages. The new converts slowly started accepting the Christian message that discouraged headhunting and drinking the traditional *zao*. Performing older religious rituals that involved appeasing local gods were condemned as idolatry, and animal sacrifices were also largely abandoned. The new converts insist that these changes 'lightened their minds' and gave them the freedom to venture outside into towns without having to perform elaborate rituals when leaving the village as done in the old traditional practices (*Paupaise/Pupouchapriak*). Now they are able to attend schools, seek government employment or even conduct business with other communities in town markets.

12 Richard M. Eaton, 'Conversion to Christianity among the Nagas, 1876-1971' in *Indian Economic and Social History Review 11* (1984).

Similarly, Heraka was a strong force especially among the Zeliangrong of North Cachar Hills, Assam from the 1930s onwards due to the active religious reform movement of Gaidinliu. Unlike Christianity which rejected all symbols and traditional practices in a wholesale manner overnight, Heraka did not immediately ban all animal sacrifices. It adopted a more gradual process by first banning only the bigger animals, but over the years propagated a call for a complete ban on animal sacrifice. Scholars have attributed the impact of the scarcity of food in the Zeliangrong areas during the 1930s for espousing this ban on animal sacrifices but this perhaps is over-theorising the reform movement. Heraka was more popular amongst the Zemei as it was not a *foreign import* but based on local reform, making it easier for people to identify with it. Moreover, old traditional customs like drinking *zao*, preserving the dances and traditional dresses were seen as tradition friendly moves.

When the Christian missionaries first arrived, especially the Baptist mission, they strictly clamped down on drinking *zao* (*zu* or *madhu)* as most of them came from mid-west America where prohibitionism values were very strong. The Baptist mission banned all usage of alcohol without understanding the importance of *zao* in Zeliangrong culture and life. Thus, a line between 'Christians' and 'animists/heathens' (condemned by the missions) was drawn and even the condition for baptism was based on giving up the *zao* completely by the converts. The missions refused to acknowledge the Naga worldview where religion and culture are both intertwined and connected. This 'civilising mission' of the Christian missionaries and their arrogance towards the traditional practices was opposed by Rani Gaidinliu through her Heraka reform. In the process, it became a competing worldview in the region causing a lot of tension and misunderstanding. This also explains the deep hostilities between the early missionaries and the indigenous religious groups like Heraka and Tingkao Ragwang Chapriak (TRC).

Gaidinliu's Heraka and its Uneasy Relationship with the Naga Insurgents

Christianity played an important role in the relationship between the Nagas and India. The blame for fostering independence was squarely put on the Christian missionaries. Nehru reiterated these accusations when he said that some Nagas who converted to Christianity became educated to some extent and because of this they joined politics and became leaders. He accused the British of encouraging these Nagas to claim independence as their last mischievous act before leaving India.[13] This was true to some extent as the impact of Christianity played a crucial role in forging a Naga identity. There is no denying that the missionaries started translating the Bible into the local language using the Roman alphabet. They opened schools that taught the Nagas to read and write in English. The schools brought the different Naga groups together where they could come and communicate intelligibly through English or Nagamese (a pidgin of Assamese, Hindi and the local dialect). The former headhunters/warriors got an education and became leaders of their community. This led to a feeling of ethnic identity and oneness giving rise to their 'imagined political community'.[14] Christianity became the rallying point of this yearning. Hence it was not surprising that the Naga rebels internalised this desire and incorporated them in their goals of an independent Christian state as seen in their later slogan of 'Nagaland for Christ'.

---

13 Pieter Steyn, *Zapuphizo: Voice of the Nagas* (London: Kegan Paul, 2002).

14 Benedict Anderson, *Imagined Communities: Reflections on the Origin and Spread of Nationalism* (London: Verso, 1991).

In the period between India's Independence and during the troubled times before and after the creation of Nagaland statehood, a Christian revival took place that transformed the very idea of Naga identity. Traditional clothes, necklaces, beads, wood carvings, and all other symbols of old Naga traditional practices were burnt publicly as a sign of shedding 'old clothes' and taking on 'the body of Christ'. This led to the loss of traditional culture overnight. Their aim was to move away from their 'past' lives and towards a promising future.

While these activities were going on in many parts of Naga-inhabited areas, the Heraka led by Rani Gaidinliu was consciously reforming their traditions to counter the threat of Christian missions. The slogan 'Loss of Culture, Loss of Identity' became popular as a counter response to the strategy of the missionaries. They were also driven by excesses of a certain form of Christianity with its emphasis on active evangelisation among the Heraka. And for this, there was no better target for their propaganda than Rani Gaidinliu, questioning her loyalty to 'Nagas' and calling her an agent of 'Hindu' India. This was further exacerbated by the hegemonic underground group of Naga rebels due to their overt Christian slogan 'Nagaland for Christ'. As mentioned earlier in the book, Gaidinliu countered this by stating that she was both a Naga and an Indian. She felt that freedom should be for all Nagas and proselytising in any form must be discouraged.

Meanwhile the 'elite' Christians saw Gaidinliu and her traditional religion as representing all that was 'satanic' and 'superstitious' compared to the Christian gospel. However, in the Heraka worldview, Rani Gaidinliu stood for all that was glorious about Naga culture, while embracing of Christianity constituted a violent rejection of all past religious beliefs and practices. With extreme condemnation and isolation meted out by the now majority Christians (it is estimated that more than 90 per cent of Nagas are Christians) to the 'non-Christians', especially to the followers of Heraka, Gaidinliu decided to fight for a separate Zeliangrong Homeland. This move has been opposed even by the current set of Naga political groups. To this end, they have been taking some deliberate steps, such as giving recognition to Zemei, Liangmei and Rongmei as separate tribes, and de-recognising the civil societies which represent the combined united groups like the Zeliangrong Baudi, All Zeliangrong Students Union, etc., from all their forums like the

Naga Hoho, ANSAM, UNC, etc. The old 'divide and rule' strategy of the British has been blatantly deployed once again. These actions can be seen as an outcome of the continued deep ideological divide between those who stand for Zeliangrong unity and those for the pan-Naga independence group. Perhaps the time has come for both parties to understand that being Indian is not antithetical to being Naga. But the question is how many of the leaders in the current setup will follow the old Gaidinliu formula that one can be both a Naga and an Indian like one can be an Assamese and an Indian or for that matter, both a Bengali and an Indian.

Heraka's Relationship with Hindu Groups

Many writers on Heraka tend to see its relationship with Hindu groups as a project to include tribal cultures and its varied traditions into one overwhelming 'Hindu Solidarity' as a strategy that has been part of the Vishwa Hindu Parishad (VHP) and Rashtriya Swayamsevak Sangh (RSS). Whether it is just speculation or a well-thought-out strategy, it is a fact that from the 1960s onwards, the Sangh Parivar through its various organisations like the VHP and Kalyan Ashram/Vanvasi Kalyan Ashram started work among the non-Christian

Nagas, primarily the Heraka, and defended them against Christian proselytising. The VHP group was the first Hindu organisation to make contact with Rani Gaidinliu who saw in her not only a great freedom fighter but also a propounder of the true 'Sanatan Dharma' in her reform movement of Heraka. They provided both moral and logistical support to the Heraka organisation. In a way, the Heraka proponents accepted what they thought was a support line in their struggles against the well-oiled machinery of proselytisation of the dominant Christian missionaries. Gradually the rhetoric of nation-building and defence against foreign culture of the VHP seeped into Heraka's propaganda and talks. Phrases like 'all religions have truth, compassion and love and are like streams that go into one big ocean', or 'invasion of foreign religion and foreign culture will bring total destruction of Naga society, so beware of this danger', became common refrains during talks and preachings. Writers tended to misinterpret the presence of Hindu symbols like *Om* and the *Swastika*, distributed by the VHP activists, which slowly found their way into the Heraka homes. Perhaps, the presence of such symbolism gave the impression that an assimilation process into the larger Hindutva project by the Hindu groups was a strategy. In actuality, the Heraka adherents were adapting these symbols to mark them off from the largely Christian population.

The entry of the Vanvasi Kalyan Ashram into the scene from the 1970s onwards in the Zeliangrong areas of the three states further strengthened the bond between the mainstream Hindu groups and the Heraka group. They acknowledged Rani Gaidinliu and Haipou Jadonang as great freedom fighters of India along with other icons of the country. They also tried to establish linkages between North East India and the rest of the larger Hindu society. Vedic proponents like Stephen Knapp even went to the extent of claiming that Arjuna from the *Mahabharata* had married a Naga wife, Ulupi, in Nagaland.[15] Writers and scholars also tried to link Gaidinliu's script with 'ancient Gupta Brahmi...which were in use throughout India some 2,500 years back,' quoting Dr Wakankar, a renowned Indian archeologist. The fables of the *Nangalog* popularised by writers like J.H. Hutton were also conveniently quoted. However, no serious historical studies were undertaken to substantiate such claims.

15 Stephen Knapp, 'My Northeast India Mission of 2003-4' (2006), www.stephen-knapp.com/my_northeast_india_mission_.htm.

Though there is no concrete evidence to prove the linkage of the Heraka with the larger Hindu cosmology, its support by the VHP, Kalyan Ashram and other Sangh Parivar organisations has led to the understanding that this is an attempt to 'Hinduise' the Heraka and show it as part of the greater Hindu society. However, there is no doubt that this symbiotic relationship has definitely led to the strengthening of the Heraka movement while keeping its indigenous identity intact. The bridge that acted as a link between the Heraka followers and the wider Hindu organisations was Rani Gaidinliu. She found supportive allies in the VHP and the Kalyan Ashram organisations in her struggle for her fledgling indigenous religious movement, the Heraka. This symbiotic relationship was solidified when Rani Gaidinliu and her Heraka leaders attended the World Hindu Conference organised by the Vishwa Hindu Parishad at Allahabad between 25-27 January 1979. Here she met Ashok Singhal, the president of the VHP, and remained in touch ever since. Rani Gaidinliu also attended the Matru Sammelan which was organised as part of the conference. Rani Gaidinliu as the president of the function gave a speech in her own dialect which was translated by Ramkui Newme, the then general secretary of the Zeliangrong Heraka Association.

This particular function coincided with the birthday of the Rani and it was celebrated with the distribution of sweets among all the attendees. This interaction paved the way for a relationship between the two groups that continues to be maintained even today.

Impact of the Heraka on the Social and Economic Life of the People

The Heraka movement of Rani Gaidinliu appealed to the people because it combined the emotional appeal with the devising of practical reform as they focused on Zeliangrong religious practices and economic problems. When the reform focused on the rituals connected with the *jhum* agricultural cycle which involved a series of animal sacrifices, or on the imposition of 'non-working days' called *neube* or *neimei* which were seen as an impediment during hard times, it appealed to the adherents as something which could free them from such burdensome practices. The old traditional practices involved many sacrifices to be made to propitiate the various smaller gods and deities and ensure a good crop. Now they have to adhere to only one Supreme God who is all powerful as Heraka reform abolished all forms of sacrifices by its insistence on achieving 'purity'.

Old practices like the giving of 'feast of merit' or *bamrumei* (in Rongmei) which aim to gain social status by displaying and sharing one's wealth with the rest of the community led to draining of resources in the society as a whole. Giving such a 'feast of merit' also involves elaborate ceremonies such as erecting of monoliths and construction of large houses (*taraangkai*) apart from the feast itself. Moreover, these feasts are followed by long periods of *neube* (prohibition) on various economic and social activities as well as travelling outside the villages. Hence if anyone has any work or travelling to do he or she has to perform elaborate rituals to propitiate the deities which usually involves animal sacrifices. Even cure for illnesses is sought through propitiation of the concerned deity usually through animal sacrifices. The above description provides a glimpse of the redundant economic practices but many other practices of *nrei, neube, neimei,* etc., led to restrictions on the movement of people outside the demarcated geographical area which may be a family home, village zone or the entire village.

The Heraka saw these old practices as limiting the movability of the villager for education, jobs and business and understood that these old ways were ill equipped to deal with the modern world. The Gaidinliu movement responded to this problem by eliminating the tradition of animal sacrifices and with it the restriction on people's movement. Hence the ban on sacrifices led to economic benefits which attracted the followers as they realised the cost effectiveness of abandoning sacrifices and feasts of merit. The doing away of *nrei, neube, neimei,* etc., led to easing of restrictions and prohibitions on the individuals to go outside for education, jobs and business. Now the Heraka people could venture out of the village, get educated and find jobs. Substituting or gradually altering the sacrificial practices, as mentioned by Pautanzan Newme, like adopting sacrifice of chicken and smaller birds instead of big animals like cattle or pigs made it more practical. So, in a sense, the Heraka was a modernising movement as it took the practical realities into account while adopting to a new worldview. For Rani Gaidinliu, the education of her people formed a very important part of her social reform movement. Many of the Heraka followers had their education sponsored by organisations like the Kalyan Ashram, sending the students outside to various cities of India on free scholarships. Becoming a doctor or an engineer was now a reality for the Heraka followers.

The introduction of the concept of the 'pure' as distinct from the 'impure' in the daily lives of the Heraka followers led to certain positive consequences like better hygiene, resulting in better health for the community as a whole. For instance, the symbolism of clean mind and body led to cleaning oneself before attending prayers in the *Kalum Kai* or *Kelumki*. On *Jalua* day, cleaning of houses and living areas including the common area of the families led to better cleanliness and hygiene. Earlier, due to prevalent *nrei, neimei, neube*, etc., people sometimes could not even clean their utensils as usage of water or working in the house was banned by unreasonable prohibitions leading to spread of diseases and illness due to such unhealthy practices. The urge for purity through actual implementation of cleanliness in mind and body as propounded by the Heraka led to better health in the Heraka villages of North Cachar Hills.

Rani Gaidinliu made the cosmology of the Zeliangrong religion a simpler one through the Heraka reform by giving primacy to Tingwang/ Tingkao Ragwang who now inherited all the attributes of the lesser gods. This led to the marginalisation of the traditional village priest who acted as a medium of the lesser gods in favour of the *paipeu,* the village elder/head. Gaidinliu saw these as a necessary positive change if the Heraka is to thrive in a modern changing society.

Maintaining a balance between the various dominant religious traditions like Christianity and Hinduism, while drawing attention to their own traditions, makes the Heraka an important and significant indigenous religious movement of India. Rani Gaidinliu's influence on and contribution to the movement remains significant.

EPILOGUE

The life of Rani Gaidinliu shows that one should never give up hope on any dream that one sets out to achieve whatever the odds may be. Her life is an example of commitment and sacrifice to her cause. She led her life with discipline, dedication, practicality, positivity and optimism in everything she did. Rani Gaidinliu shook the establishment of her times with her courage, bravery and her attitude to fight for her rights. Her sense of justice and humane approach to all obstacles that she faced inspired her supporters and her people to rise up against the mighty oppressors like the British colonial rulers. Her love for her own culture, traditional ways of life, strong belief that the indigenous way of life was the best option for her people and not the foreign proselytising religions and alien lifestyle, which were seen as an imposition by the colonial power, inspired her reformation movement.

This conviction helped organise her traditional religious group into a well-structured 'Heraka' (pure religion) and inspired groups such as the Tingkao Ragwang Chapriak (TRC) to organise themselves in a modern setting to withstand the onslaught of the all-pervading, alien proselytising religions.

In trying to tell the story of the great Rani Gaidinliu, many scholars have tried to project her as a political figurehead who fought against the colonial powers as part of the great freedom struggle for India's Independence. Though this assessment may be partially correct, it is seen from the story of her life as told here that it is not quite as simple. Her story was about a fight against injustice which was forced upon her oppressed people and how she was inspired by her mentor Jadonang whose movement was unfortunately nipped in the bud by the British. Gaidinliu's story is also about how divine inspiration can bring about change and help people to unite and stand up against exploitation and injustice. She is a symbol against alien Westernised culture and she has brought back pride to tribal identity through dances, songs, hymns, dresses and traditional jewelleries which have inculcated a strong sense of pride in one's culture and tradition. Gaidinliu's movement inspired the whole spectrum of indigenous movement, especially in North East India, and she became a backbone against the bulwark of the proselytising religious groups.

But in trying to bring about change through her socio-religious reform movement, she paid a heavy price personally. Because of her strong stand for her indigenous religion, she came under a vicious attack from the Christian missionaries' groups which were already starting to be entrenched amongst her Zeliangrong people and the tribals in general in North East India. The Naga undergrounds who were also adherents of the Christian missionaries' work condemned her movement and made life difficult for her and her followers. When they failed to persuade her to join them, attempts were made to even eliminate her physically, forcing her to go underground once again in independent India to protect herself and her followers. For a long time, since her release from jail by the Assam government, she was deliberately ignored and all kinds of wild and baseless rumours about her religion, terming it as a cult, were spread by her opponents. She was a victim of a systematic vilification campaign by the missionaries of those times. So much so that, many of her family members and villagers disowned her and did not want to be associated with her. Her decision to work in the Cachar hills in Assam amongst the Zemei brought about a drastic change in the region. However, her religious reform movement was not allowed to take off in the Zeliangrong areas of Manipur and Nagaland where the missionaries had by the 1960s and 70s become well entrenched and organised. A remnant of the indigenous religious movement managed to survive in the Imphal valley as the valley had a plural setup and mixed population. The TRC movement managed to survive and even thrive inspired by Jadonang and Gaidinliu's movement. The TRC have embraced the songs composed by both Jadonang and Gaidinliu in their hymn books and continue to look up to them in their various rituals, prayers, dances and songs.

But what exactly is the present status of the 'Zeliangrong Homeland', which was the dream of Haipou Jadonang and Rani Gaidinliu? As mentioned elsewhere in the book, the opposition from the Naga Nationalist Political Groups (NNPGs) when the ceasefire and the talks started in the mid-90s forced the Zeliangrong People's Convention (ZPC) which was spearheading the homeland movement to be kept in abeyance on the understanding that a fair deal will be given to the

Zeliangrong group when the agreement is signed with the Government of India. But the way the talks are headed now, it seems quite clear that the sovereignty issue, over which the NNC and later on the NSCN groups differed ideologically with Rani Gaidinliu and even fought with each other with loss of many lives on both sides, may now be coming together whatever the semantics used by the groups involved in the negotiations may be. As the mist clears, Rani Gaidinliu's stand that it is possible to be both a proud Naga and a proud Indian is after all slowly being accepted.

APPENDICES

Appendix – I

Jug-Neipuiluh *of Haipou Jadonang (Psalm of Glory)*
Rongmei Text and English Rendering

Ragwang Damtuang Meinung renraye
God's ordained Worldly life worries me,
Ringpui Jug[1] *Tio*
Give us the Jug of life,
Tan roi mangna Tubam nie
I want a life of ease, free from all toil and labour
Rale Tilou Jaio,
Oh God, give us soon
Ndi bangtho kangim kanga ye, Ai ping bamtonge
The world underneath is rumbling, I am afraid
Tingkao thumei Latmu gai e, Ai Laniye
Heaven's everlasting words are good, I like them
Apou Ragwang pankhaurui Gwang tuni ye[2]

---

1 *Jug* is a corrupted word from the Sanskrit word *Yug* meaning age or time or a period of extended time, but Jadonang used 'Jug' in the sense of glorious times or glory of time. This hymn is the most popular of Haipou Jadonang's songs.

2 *Gwang tuni ye* literally means to be enthroned as king. But enthronement as king is better understood as redemption of one's soul, spiritual redemption.

With God's grace, wish to be redeemed
Atao kulana, Ansei Ragwang lun houlana, athuan Gwang Tuniye
Praying now, seeing God today, wish to be redeemed tomorrow
Ragwang Nangkai[3] *gai e, nanglun gaichui ye*
Oh God, Your Abode is beautiful, Your good self is more beautiful
Manseita damme, manseita damme
Man is ordained, Man is ordained
Ragwang Kaiku[4] *meigoi Meitheimangna gaironne*
Whoever prays at the abode of God will be blessed and immortal,
Mansei khang gai e, Mansei khang gai e
Good for mankind, good for mankind
Ai Ringniye penrarijo, ragwang gaimei le
I want to live, spare me from any evil, Oh good God
Gaitong Ti o, Di sinlem bamniye
Bless me I want to rule the world
Ragwang pankhourui, Ragwang Pankhourui
With the grace of God, with the grace of God
Tingkaotho samniye, bamkei nimakge
Wish to fly to the Heaven, don't like to be confined
Ragwang kaikhou Bamkeimeirui ringsaan Gwang tukhang
Whoever remains at the abode of God will be redeemed
Gaiye Ragwang kaihei, meiring puisan kuniye Gwang tikhang
Beautiful is God's Abode, I wish to see it for eternity and be redeemed
Aita aojen lumsanni, Ragwang Kummang ronne
None is more kind than God Himself

3 *Ragwang kai*: God's house may be interpreted as Heaven or Abode of God.

4 *Ragwang kaiku*: Ascending to God's abode is interpreted as praying to God.

Kakhang gaimei goinu Ragwangkai ku mangronne
Well-to-do, do not pray and worship God
Mansei Kakhang sprang khourui Ragwang kai kutonge
Suffering men worship God
Jug neinina[5] *kupu tonge*
I pray for the Jug
Tingkao Ragwang,
Oh Heavenly God,
Apou Ragwangle
Oh My God
Apou Baomeile
Oh my Almighty Lord.

5 The last stanza of the song was added to the main as revealed by God to Muhpui Meilaona of Fulertal in Cachar, Assam.

Appendix – II

Letter from Lady Astor
London, May 10, 1939

Dear Pandit Jawaharlal Nehru,
You will remember that last summer you spoke to me about the case of Gaidinliu, the girl of the Naga clan who was imprisoned in 1933, in connection with the murder of some Manipuri travellers in 1930. I have had a certain amount of correspondence with the India Office about her case, and they have made some investigations as a result, and sent me a good deal of detailed information. To put it briefly I am told that a man named Jadonang set himself up as a sort of Messiah, and that Gaidinliu was his Priestess; the murder referred to appear to be a kind of sacrifice to Gods of Jadonang's religion. It was feared that the whole tribe, the Kukis, were in danger of massacre from the Naga followers of this cult. It is stated that there was ample evidence of Gaidinliu's implication in the murders, and it was only her youth and the fact of Jadonang's influence over her which caused the Court to commute the death sentence.

It is added that the movement among the Nagas has not yet died down, and would break if she is released, and that she is at present considered a 'potent source of danger to the peace of Manipur State and the Province of Assam'.

The Secretary of State stresses the fact that the matter of Gaidinliu's sentence is one for the Crown Representative and that as the question relates to the internal affairs of Manipur and not to British territory, he is not prepared to question His Excellency's discretion.

In answer to my representation asking if, for such a young girl, constructive reformation treatment would not be more beneficial in its effect than imprisonment, especially now that the influence of Jadonang is removed, I have been informed that a modified form of Borstal treatment with facilities for education is adopted in Assam Jail. I have been further assured that my suggestions with regard to Gaidinliu's case shall be passed on to the Crown Representative for consideration. I do hope that some good will come out of my efforts, though I am sorry that the business has taken so long. I hope your daughter and sister are better.

Yours Sincerely,
Nancy Astor

{Gaidinliu, a Naga girl, was sentenced to life imprisonment. There had been a Naga uprising. She was a young girl of about twenty and it shocked me that this should have happened and I took up her case}[1]

1 Jawaharlal Nehru, *Bunch of Old Letters* (Bombay: Asia Publishing House, 1958).

Appendix - III

Letter to Lady Astor

Allahabad, May 27, 1939

Dear Lady Astor,

Thank you for your letter of 10th May in which you told me about the steps you took regarding Gaidinliu, the girl of the Naga clan in Assam. The information I have received does not tally with the account that the India Office has supplied you. The girl must be an unusually interesting person if she is still supposed to be a "potent source of danger to the peace of Manipur State and the province of Assam". I should have thought that the peace of Manipur State and the Province of Assam had a very insecure foundation if it rested on a girl in her twenties to be kept in prison indefinitely.

I am grateful to you for all the trouble you have taken in this matter.

Yours Sincerely,

Sd/-

Jawaharlal Nehru

Appendix – IV

Agreement and Statement of Negotiation between Rani Gaidinliu Party and D.C. Kohima on 5th and 6th January, 1966

Leader of the party said: The Zeliangrong people has been helping the Indian National Congress Party right from the British time ie 1925 upto date. Shri Jadonang lost his life for the cause of the country. Rani Gaidinliu was actively helping the Congress Government. In spite of all these helps, Indian Congress Government has not given or done anything for the Zeliangrong. But the people who did not at all help the Congress Government have now got separate States etc. Why the Government has not given anything for Zeliangrong in recognition of its assistance to the Congress Party, for this reason alone we have all gone underground.

1. *The leader further said :-* Zemei, Liangmei and Rongmei tribes now covering the North Cachar Hills, Assam, Manipur and Nagaland should form a separate district with the name Zeliangrong. They further assured that they are prepared to provide 2000 soldiers to fight for the country from the Zeliangrong district.

Answer of the DC party:- This is a political issue and the Deputy Commissioner is not in a position to give answer in any way. However, if they feel strongly about it, then they are advised to come out and represent their demand to the Government. The DC further impressed that they could not attain their objective by remaining in the jungle.

Decision arrived at by Rani Party after a long discussion and explanation given by the Deputy Commissioner.

The Rani Party agreed that they will not make it a precondition for surrender but when they come overground, they will still keep on demanding Zeliangrong district comprising of Zemei, Liangmei and Rongmei people living in Cachar district (Assam), Tamenglong (Manipur) and Peren Sub-division (Nagaland) in a non-violent, constitutional way and Government should agree to this in writing that none of the people demanding the said district be harassed by the government.

2. The Rani Party want a separate force of their own with the post under the name of rani and they should be given rank as far as possible commensurate with their qualification, suitability and availability of vacancies.

Answer: The Deputy Commissioner replied that the force has to be under one of the two Battalions. As regards keeping the name of Rani associated with the force, the same will be referred to the Government for decision. If agreed by the Government, the name of the force may be named 1st Bn. SNAP (Rani Party).

Decision arrived at by the Rani Party after discussion and explanation by the DC:

The reply given by the DC if agreed to by the Government should be given to Rani Party in writing and also the Rani Force under 1st Bn SNAP should be kept in Zeliangrong area. They will, however be ready to go anywhere and serve when their service are required in any emergency.

3. All the criminal cases pending against the Rani Party should be dropped. Rani Party also will not file any case against anybody. The DC agreed to put up the matter to the Government.

4. In the event of the Rani Party surrendering with all armed personnel with arms, grouping of the five villages as envisaged should be dropped. The DC agreed to put up to the Government.

5. A post should be opened to Nzauna to protect the five villages. The DC replied that this may not be possible. However, he agreed to put up to the Government.

6. It was also agreed that if the Government agreed to all points, they will bring out all armed personnel of the North Cachar Hills, Tamenglong and Peren sub-division including Rani. The strength of the Force, arms, ammunitions etc will be disclosed on 15th January, 1966 morning to the Deputy Commissioner when he will meet Rani. This will be followed by surrender on the same day.

Note: All possible arrangement for Rani's safety will be made by the Government. She should be given her pension with retrospective effect and she should be allowed to settle down anywhere in Indian Union under protection.

The above discussion took place on 5th and 6th January, 1966 at Tening, Nagaland between the leaders of Rani Party consisting of the following:

- *Hewrangding (Brigadier)*
- *Dingam, Dy. Commissioner*

- *Hewzai (Major)*
- *Irangheung (Subedar)*
- *Ramga (Captain)*
- *Ireheung (Major)*

The Team of Deputy Commissioner, Kohima district consisting of the following officers and public leaders :-

- *Col. D.K. Roy, Comdt. 1st SNAP*
- *T.P. Imchen, Extra Asst. Commissioner, Peren*
- *D.B. Thapa, Circle Officer, Tening*
- *Subba, Circle Officer, Kohima*
- *Ikeshing, Head Dobhasi*
- *Namgangheing, Tribal Council Chairman, (TCC)*
- *Huthonbou, Tribal Council Member*
- *Songha, Tribal Council Member*

Appendix - V

Declaration on Zeliangrong Homeland, Tamenglong

30th November, 1982

Whereas fully aware of the common ancestry and cultural identity of the Zeliangrong people of the great Naga family having occupied a compact territory along the Barail mountain and its southern ranges of North East India, living from time immemorial in traditional village republics with complete control over land and maintaining political relationship with the neighbouring peoples of Meiteis, Dimasas and other Nagas.

Having refused to reconcile with the British Colonial rule and fragmentation of our land and people into three administrative units of Manipur, North Cachar Hills and Nagaland;

Having been dissatisfied at the continuation of the colonial by free India and having denied the opportunity of living together under a single political roof despite a long standing demand for reunification of our scattered population and fragmented territories;

We do solemnly affirm that it is the inalienable right of the Zeliangrong people to determine our political future and to secure to ourselves the political liberty, social justice and equal economic opportunities guaranteed under the Constitution of India.

Whereas recalling the heroic struggle of the Zeliangrong in the National liberation movement during which we fought against the British Government under the leadership of our leaders Haipou Jadonang and Rani Gaidinliu who were inspired by the Civil Disobedience Movement of Mahatma Gandhi and our love for freedom, which we always regard as our birthright;

Having been completely disillusioned at being denied to enjoy the fruits of India's freedom due to the Government of India's continuous refusal to take cognisance of the Zeliangrong problem and the rejection of our legitimate demand for political integration for which we fought the aliens rulers;

We feel that in independent India, our dream has not been redeemed and that freedom of India has come to mean to the Zeliangrong people as a mere change of masters;

Whereas the British policy of balkanising the Zeliangrong territories into three states of Assam, Manipur and Nagaland had not only obstructed the achievement of the political, economic, social and educational progress but had threatened the very identity of the Zeliangrong;

The policy of isolation, exploitation and neglect of our people is unfortunately continued even in independent India of today in the three states.

The political and administrative balkanisations have reduced our people into political minorities, thus denying to us the greater opportunity which would have been possible if we were in a single political unit. The Zeliangrong people have been artificially made minorities wherever they are and exploited in administrative and economic fronts by the more advanced sections of the other populations and the civil services are manned and controlled by irresponsible state bureaucrats and consequently making our people extremely poor and educationally backward and completely neglected. The economic development programmes so far introduced in our areas are not suited to the Zeliangrong ethos and has not resulted in the integrated economic growth of the Zeliangrong people. It is sad but true that the Zeliangrong areas are amongst the most backward regions of India's North East.

Whereas in the creation of administrative units during the British rule or in the formation of the states and the formation of the political processes in North East India in post independent period affecting the Zeliangrong areas and people, no attempt was made to ascertain the opinion, consent or mandate of the Zeliangrong people, neither in the merger of Manipur with the dominion of India in 1949 nor in the creation of Nagaland state, and the demand for integration of the Zeliangrong people was not considered while granting full statehood to Manipur in1972;

Realising that our associations with the States of Manipur, Assam and Nagaland have failed to fulfil the aspiration of the Zeliangrong;

We solemnly declare that the political and administrative arrangements, which were created without our consent against our wish are not binding on our people for perpetuity and that the time has come to dissolve the political bands that bind us with the three states in peaceful and smooth process.

Whereas fully realising our identity, political unity, economic progress, social justice and cultural values cannot be protected unless we live in a single homeland where our people and our representatives would take part in the decision making process both in the legislative and executive level;

Also fully conscious of the opportune moment to act boldly to shape our political future for the generation to come at this critical juncture of our history;

Having discussed the issue in depth and reviewed the progress of the demand for Zeliangrong Homeland as raised by different organisations and leaders;

We, the representatives of the Zeliangrong people of the three states endorsed the formation of the Zeliangrong people's Convention to lead the movement for a common homeland for Zeliangrong people. The creation of the Homeland shall enable the Zeliangrong people to enjoy political freedom, preserve our identity, our social and moral values, ensure economic progress and protect our land, forest, our customs and tradition.

We assure that equal treatment and protection shall be provided to all citizens and communities in the proposed state irrespective of number, language, religion and caste.

We urge the government and people of India to create the state for Zeliangrong people on the principle of protecting and safeguarding the legitimate rights and aspirations of smaller nationalities and ethnic minorities which should be made a permanent feature of India's federal political system. We also believe that there is need for the reorganisation of states in India on this principle without jeopardising the country's unity and integrity.

We appeal to all the liberal and progressive forces in India to support the demand of the Zeliangrong state, which is interwoven with the universal struggle for the upliftment of the millions of downtrodden people throughout the nation. We also appeal to all the people living in the Zeliangrong areas irrespective of caste, language and religion to support the cause.

We reaffirm our belief in the ideals of democracy, secularism, socialism enshrined in the Indian Constitution.

We do hereby authorise the Zeliangrong People's Convention (ZPC) as the sole representative body to take up the necessary action for the achievement of our political objective and affirm that the ZPC shall use constitutional, peaceful and democratic means in this struggle for our homeland within Indian Union.

We also appeal to all the Zeliangrong people to extend all their support to the ZPC till our goal is achieved and call upon leaders, intellectuals and the common masses in the villages to prepare for the coming struggle.

On this thirtieth Day of the month of November, one thousand nine hundred eighty-two, Anno Domino (A.D.), the following delegates and representatives attending the Fourth Conference of the ZPC at Tamenglong do hereby in the name of Almighty God append our signatures of approval to this solemn declaration.

Zeliangrong Rintelou!

Sd/-
(RANI GAIDINLIU)
President, ZPC

Sd/-
(INCHEKAMBE)
Vice-President, ZPC

Sd/-
(KALANLUNG KAMEI)
Vice President, ZPC

Sd/-
(N.C. ZELIANG)
Vice President, ZPC

Sd/-
(N. PAUHEU)
Vice President, ZPC

Sd/-
(PROF. GANGMUMEI KAMEI)
General Secretary, ZPC

REFERENCES

All Zeliangrong Students' Union, Assam, Manipur & Nagaland. 2009. *A Brief Account of Zeliangrong Nagas.*

Anderson, Benedict. 1991. *Imagined Communities: Reflection on the Origin and Spread of Nationalism*. London: Verso.

Bower, Ursula Graham. 2003. *Naga Path*. Guwahati/Delhi: Spectrum Publication.

Dev, S.C. 1988. *Nagaland: The Untold Story*. Kolkata: Gouri Dev.

Eaton, Richard M. 1984. 'Conversion to Christianity among the Nagas, 1876-1971'. *Indian Economic and Social History Review*, vol. 11.

Grierson, G.A., ed. 1904. *Linguistic Survey of India*, vol. 3, *Tibeto-Burman Family*, Pt. 3. Calcutta: Superintendent of Government Printing.

Kamei, Gangmumei. 2004. *A History of the Zeliangrong Nagas: From Makhel to Rani Gaidinliu*. Guwahati/Delhi: Spectrum Publication.

-----. 2009. *Jadonang: A Mystic Naga Rebel.* Imphal: G. Lanshailu Kamei.

-----. 2006. *Essays on Primordial Religion*. New Delhi: Akansha.

-----. 2005. *Tingkao Ragwang Chapriak: The Zeliangrong Primordial Religion.* Assam, Manipur & Nagaland: TRC Phom.

Longkumer, Arkotong. 2016. *The Poetry of Resistance – The Heraka Movement of North East India.* Guwahati: NESRC.

-----. 2016. 'Lines That Speak'. *HAU: Journal of Ethnographic Theory* 6(2): 123-147.

Mills, J.P. 1932. 'A Note on Gaidinliu's Movement'. Kohima.

Miri, Sujata. 1991. *Liangmai Nagas: Legends and Stories.* New Delhi: Vikas Publishing.

Nehru, Jawaharlal. 1958. *Bunch of Letters*. Bombay: Asia Publishing House.

Newme, Pautanzan. 2015. 'Mystical Early Life of Ranima Gaidinliu till the Arrest of Jadonang' (unpublished).

-----. 2001. 'Origin and Reformation of Heraka Religion'. In *Heraka Golden Jubilee Souvenir* magazine.

-----. 2015. 'History of Padma Bhushan Ranima Gaidinliu, the Freedom Fighter of India'. In *The Flame of Fire (100 Years Birth Celebration 1915-2015)*. North East Bharat: Zeliangrong Heraka Association.

Newme, Widonlule, trans. 2019. *Tingwang Hingde*. Zeliangrong Heraka Association, North East India.

Pamei, Namthiubuiyang. 2001. *Trail from Makuilongdi: The Continuing Saga of the Zeliangrong People*. Tamenglong, Manipur: Gironta Charitable Foundation.

Parrat, Saroj N. Arambam, and John Parrat. 1995. 'Kabui Messiah: The Jadonang Movement in Manipur'. *Internationales Asien Forum*, vol. 26, nos. 3-4: 285-302.

Pemberton, R.B. 1835. *Report on the Eastern Frontier of British India*.

Reid, Robert. 1942. *History of the Frontier Areas Bordering on Assam*. Guwahati/Delhi: Spectrum Publication.

Rustomji, N.K. 1971. *Enchanted Frontier*. Bombay.

Sen, S.P. 1972. *Dictionary of National Biography: Note on Rani Gaidinliu by Gangmumei Kamei*. Calcutta: Indian Institute of Historical Studies.

Singh, N. Joykumar. 1992. *Socialist Movements in Manipur (1917-1951)*. New Delhi: Mittal Publications.

Singh, K.S. 1983. *Tribal Movements in India*. New Delhi: Manohar Publishers.

Steyn, Pieter. 2002. *Zapuphizo: Voice of the Nagas*. London: Kegan Paul.

Yonuo, Asoso. 1984. *The Naga Struggle Against the British under Jadonang and Rani Gaidinliu*. Kohima: self published.

Zeliang, N.C. 1998. *Zeliangrong Heraka Preacher Handbook*. Zeliangrong Heraka Association (Assam, Manipur & Nagaland).

ACKNOWLEDGEMENTS

A book on a person as public and controversial as Rani Gaidinliu shades the difference between self and society, biography and history. I have tried to stay as close to the central characters as possible. I have not suppressed facts or been coy with opinion but as the saying goes, the interpretation is in the telling.

My father Prof. Gangmumei Kamei was a close friend of the Rani and, in fact, the responsibility of writing on the life of Rani Gaidinliu fell on me after the sudden demise of my father while serving his term as Member, North Eastern Council (NEC) at Shillong in 2017. He was planning to publish a collection of articles by different scholars and writers on Rani Gaidinliu, edited by him. The collected work was rather in a disjointed form as many writers were not academicians and some of the articles were taken out as extracts from others' works/books. My sister Dr Jenpuiru Kamei suggested that I should write a biography on Rani Gaidinliu instead. My father's existing material could be supplemented with my own research on the subject. My Ama (mother) and wife Ayang encouraged me to take up the challenge and dedicate my work to my late father.

For this work to see the light of day, I would like to acknowledge the contributions of many individuals and groups. I would like to thank Shri Abuan Kamei, former private secretary to Rani Gaidinliu, whom I have been interacting with over the years on many matters related to the Rani. I am grateful to Shri Ramkuiwangbe Newme from Lodiram village, Haflong (now Dima Hasao district) in Assam. His deep understanding of the Heraka religion threw light on the Rani's ideas about indigenous religion and how it shaped its response to the greater outside world. Valuable inputs have been provided by Shri Chaoba Kamson, general secretary of the Tingkao Ragwang Chapriak (TRC), on the impact of Rani Gaidinliu in the development and evolving of TRC as an organised religion.

I would like to thank Miss Tasile Zeliang from Jalukie for generously sharing her many collections of photos on Ranima and writeups on Heraka. I sincerely thank my well-wisher Shri Huruiji whose constant encouragement and company made my various visits to Jalukie and Peren possible to meet people connected with the book. My uncle Shri Chamkandai Kamei despite being more than 75 years old willingly accompanied me and even outpaced me in our climb to the Bhubon cave in Assam's Barak Valley, the holiest site of the Zeliangrongs. I thank Shri C.R. Zeliang, a retired Indian Trade Service officer and his wife for sharing their story and graciously hosting me in Jalukie, Nagaland. Another friend who encouraged me was my childhood friend Navin Giri who kept reminding me to finish the project. I would like to thank my brothers, Dr Ram Kamei and Shyam Kamei, for their valuable feedback and suggestions.

I wish to thank Shri Jagdamba Mallji, Shri Gopal Krishna Kakkadankandy of the Kalyan Ashram, Nagaland Chapter and Shri Kedar Kulkarni of the Manipur chapter of Kalyan Ashram.

I am thankful to my private secretaries over the years, Shri Okram Nico for his valuable help while in Shillong, Shri Raktim Roy in Dibrugarh, and Shri Zasiveituo in Dimapur.

I wish to thank Trisha De Niyogi and my publisher Tultul De Niyogi who has been most generous in working out the nitty gritty of the agreement. I thank my editor Sucharita Ghosh for her patience and technical help. But this easy link-up with my publisher would not have been possible without the initial encouragement and introduction to the publishing world by my young friend Aiyushman Dutta of Guwahati who unfortunately passed away during the devastating Covid-19 pandemic. I will miss him dearly.

I would like to thank Dr Vibha Joshi Parkin, from the School of Anthropology and Museum Ethnography, Oxford University, for showing keen interest in my work and going out of her way to obtain licence/copyrights of some valuable photographs from the Pitt Rivers Museum, Oxford. I sincerely express my gratitude to the authorities at Pitt Rivers Museum, Oxford University, for not only giving me permission to use the photos of the Gaidinliu notebooks but also for waiving off the licence fee.

No man can function alone, especially a busy bureaucrat whose work schedule and tours come in the way of a normal family life. For the support system that makes it all possible, I thank my partner and wife Ayang, and my three wonderful children Elena, Arsene and Jeni. Thank you all.

The author as a baby in Rani Gaidinliu's arms at his home in Imphal in late 1972. Photo courtesy: Author

Lid with the basket made with woven plant fibre, which contains 12 notebooks of Rani Gaidinliu at the time of her capture in 1932 by the British. Photo. no. 1928.69.1570.01. Photo courtesy: Pitt Rivers Museum, Oxford

Above both: *Samples of the copy book filled with characters suggesting writings, in ink and pencil. Part of a set of 12 notebooks inside a basket. Photo no. 1928.69.1570.4. Photos courtesy: Pitt Rivers Museum, Oxford*

Images of the commemorative coin of 100 rupees (front and back) issued by the Government of India in August 2015

Images of the circulation coin of five rupees (front and back) issued by the Government of India in August 2015

OTHER PUBLISHED BOOKS
in this new series

Charu Majumdar: *The Dreamer Rebel*

Heisnam Sabitri: *The Way of the Thamoi*

Homi J Bhabha: *A Renaissance Man among Scientists*

Jamini Roy: *A Painter Who Revisited the Roots*

RK Laxman: *Back with a Punch*

Muthulakshmi Reddy: *A Trailblazer in Surgery and Women's Rights*

Sarada Devi: *Holiness, Charisma and Iconic Motherhood*